# EVIDENCE: An Exemplary Study
## *A Craig Family Case History*

by

Milton Rubincam

Special Publication No. 49

National Genealogical Society

HERITAGE BOOKS
2012

# HERITAGE BOOKS
*AN IMPRINT OF HERITAGE BOOKS, INC.*

## Books, CDs, and more—Worldwide

For our listing of thousands of titles see our website at
www.HeritageBooks.com

Published 2012 by
HERITAGE BOOKS, INC.
Publishing Division
100 Railroad Ave. #104
Westminster, Maryland 21157

Copyright © 1981 National Genealogical Society
Washington, D.C.

Library of Congress Catalog Card No. 81-86218

All rights reserved. No part of this book may be reproduced or transmitted in any form or by any means, electronic or mechanical, including photocopying, recording or by any information storage and retrieval system without written permission from the author, except for the inclusion of brief quotations in a review.

International Standard Book Numbers
Paperbound: 978-0-7884-5410-3
Clothbound: 978-0-7884-9387-4

## TABLE OF CONTENTS

| | |
|---|---:|
| *Statement of the Study* | 1 |
| Captain Samuel Craig | 3 |
| The Craig Family: General Considerations | 4 |
| The Craigs of Craig's Settlement | 4 |
| Pedigree I | 5 |
| Pedigree II | 6 |
| Pedigree III | 8 |
| Thomas Craig, Esq., of Allen Township | 8 |
| William Craig, Sheriff of Northampton County | 12 |
| General Thomas Craig | 15 |
| Hugh Craig | 19 |
| Captain Charles Craig | 19 |
| Captain William Craig | 23 |
| Daniel Craig, of Warrington Township, Bucks County, Pa. | 23 |
| Colonel Thomas Craig | 25 |
| Captain John Craig | 26 |
| Lieutenant Robert Craig | 28 |
| Conclusion | 29 |
| Revised Pedigree IV | 30 |
| Bibliography | 31 |
| Index | 39 |

# EVIDENCE: An Exemplary Study
## *A Craig Family Case History*

This study was initially made in an effort to discover the relationship, if any, between certain Revolutionary War officers named Craig who are listed in Heitman's *Historical Register of Officers of the Continental Army*.[1] One of these officers was Samuel Craig, an ancestor of the writer's client, Craig Colgate, Jr., of Washington, D.C., who made a grant to the National Genealogical Society for research on the problem and publication of the results. An intensive search has been made by Mr. Colgate, Joseph L. Graham of Philadelphia, a professional researcher, genealogist Charles R. Barker of Lansdowne, Pa., and the contributor. These researches were conducted in The National Archives in Washington, D.C., the manuscript and microfilm collections of the Genealogical and Historical Societies of Pennsylvania, Philadelphia, the Northampton County Courthouse and the Northampton County Archives Building, Easton, Pa., the Division of Archives and Manuscripts, Bureau of Archives and History, the Pennsylvania Historical and Museum Commission, Harrisburg, Pa., and in numerous other places from Albany to Richmond.

Attention was directed to Northampton County, Pennsylvania, since some of the officers entered military service there at the beginning of the Revolution. There was in that area a Scotch-Irish "Craig's Settlement." The numerous published accounts of the Craig family are confusing, contradictory, and without documentation.[2] The several Craig families in the county appear to have had a common origin for the most part, but so many members are named Thomas, William and John that it is difficult to disentangle them.

Milton Rubincam
C.G., F.A.S.G., F.N.G.S.,
F.G.S.P., F.T.S.G.S., F.U.G.A.

## 1. CAPTAIN SAMUEL CRAIG[3]

All efforts to determine the parentage of Mr. Colgate's ancestor, Samuel Craig, have failed thus far. There is no proof that he belonged to the Craig's Settlement family. The only pieces of evidence that connect him with Northampton County are his entrance into a Northampton County military unit and a Virginian's power of attorney authorizing him to sell lands in that county.

The first documentary evidence for Samuel Craig's existence is dated 25 June 1775, when he was commissioned a Third Lieutenant in Colonel William Thompson's Battalion of Riflemen, which was raised in Northampton County and convened on the village green at Easton, Pennsylvania. On the same day two other Craigs were appointed officers in the same battalion: Thomas, as Second Lieutenant, and Charles, as First Lieutenant. The battalion ultimately became the First Pennsylvania Regiment. Samuel's entire service during the Revolutionary War was with this unit. He was promoted to Second Lieutenant, 8 November 1775, First Lieutenant, 1 January 1776, and Captain, 1 October 1776. He fought in the battles of Long Island, Trenton, Brandywine (wounded), Paoli, and other actions, and he was at Valley Forge during the fateful winter of 1777-78. He retired from the Army, 17 January 1781, right after the mutiny of the Pennsylvania Line.

After the Revolution Captain Craig removed to New York and entered the stagecoach business. Some time between July 1781 and May 1782 he married Rachel, daughter of Benjamin Davies, New York master mariner and shopkeeper, by his wife Elizabeth Wessels. Their only child, Samuel Davies Craig, was born (probably in New York City), 3 January 1785.

In the following years Craig was active in buying and selling lands and acquiring free lands by virtue of his war service, including 600 acres of Donation Lands in what is now Mercer County, Pennsylvania, which he and his wife sold to John Nicholson of Philadelphia on 25 November 1794, for £281.5.0., "lawful money of Pennsylvania." Two years later the Craigs quarrelled and separated. Most of his activities were centered in New York, but on 25 April 1800 the Surveyor General of Pennsylvania appointed him Deputy Surveyor for Wayne County. He was attorney for several persons, holding powers of attorney from Frederick Molyneaux who owned lands in Kanawha County, (now West) Virginia, and John Gordon, of Alexandria, Virginia, who empowered him to sell his lands in Northampton County, Pennsylvania. In the fall of 1802 he apparently went to Philadelphia on some business and died there in the yellow fever epidemic, 22 September 1802.

Captain Samuel Craig has been widely confused with another Samuel Craig, a native of York County, Pennsylvania, who served in the Fifth Pennsylvania Regiment and afterwards in The Commander-in-Chief's Life Guard, and deserted after Yorktown.[4] Some time after the war this Samuel removed to South Carolina, and thence, to Greene County, Tennessee, where he died in 1807. Years later his widow, Jane (Innis) Craig, claimed and obtained a pension based on her husband's service *as Captain in the First Pennsylvania Regiment* (!). Her file (W348) in The National Archives is a bulky one. Her pension was granted in 1844, but suspended in 1848 when a reexamination of documents revealed that Captain Samuel Craig's wife was Rachel and not Jane. The old lady was persistent, however, and in 1852 resumed the fight, still insisting her husband was a captain in the First Pennsylvania Regiment. Surprisingly, and in spite of conflicting testimony, she was restored to the pension rolls. To add to the confusion, descendants of Samuel and Jane (Innis) Craig have joined the D.A.R. on the basis of his alleged service as a captain, not as a member of Washington's Life Guard.

## 2. THE CRAIG FAMILY: GENERAL CONSIDERATIONS

The difficulty of reconstructing the genealogy of the Craig family (or families) of Northampton, Bucks, and Montgomery Counties, Pennsylvania, lies in the absence of declarations of kinship in deeds between members of the family (or families) and in the sparsity of wills. The repetition of forenames adds to the problem; fortunately, in most cases occupations and status are given so that we can distinguish William Craig, Esquire, from William Craig, miller, and William Craig, yeoman, and Thomas Craig, Esquire, from Thomas Craig, yeoman, and so on. To further add to our problems we were unable to locate church records that might help. All of the Craigs apparently were Presbyterians.

The Continental Army officers listed in Heitman's *Historical Register* for whom we attempted to find relationships, according to Mr. Colgate's directive, are: Captain Charles, 1st Continental Infantry, and 4th Continental Dragoons; Paymaster Hugh, 11th Pennsylvania Regiment; Captain John, 2nd Pennsylvania Battalion, 3rd and 4th Pennsylvania Dragoons; 1st Lieutenant Robert, 2nd Canadian (Hazen's) Regiment, who was described as of Pennsylvania; Captain Samuel, 1st Pennsylvania Regiment, already discussed; Colonel Thomas, 3rd Pennsylvania Regiment (after the war a Major General of Militia); Regimental Quartermaster Thomas, 9th Pennsylvania; and Captain William, 3rd Pennsylvania Regiment.

## 3. THE CRAIGS OF CRAIG'S SETTLEMENT

Nothing is known of the origin of the Craig family, where they came from in Ireland, or when they came to America. They appear about 1728 in that part of Bucks County which became Northampton County on 11 March 1752. The area in which they settled was erected into Allen's Township on 10 June 1748, and was called variously "Craig's Settlement," or the "Scotch-Irish" or "Irish Settlement." The township was named for William Allen, afterwards Chief Justice of Pennsylvania and a Revolutionary War Loyalist, who had many real estate dealings with the Craigs. He is also said to have had a Craig ancestry.[5]

The contradictory lineages of the Craigs is well exemplified by consulting three accounts, two in Roberts, *et al.*, history of Lehigh County and the third in Clemens' *The Craig Family of Pennsylvania*. They are best explained in chart form:

# PEDIGREE I: ROBERTS, et al., 2:200

WILLIAM CRAIG, of Stirlingshire, Scotland, "who, to escape the persecution of the Presbyterians by James I,"[16] settled at Dungannon, Ireland: four of his sons and three daughters emigrated to America.

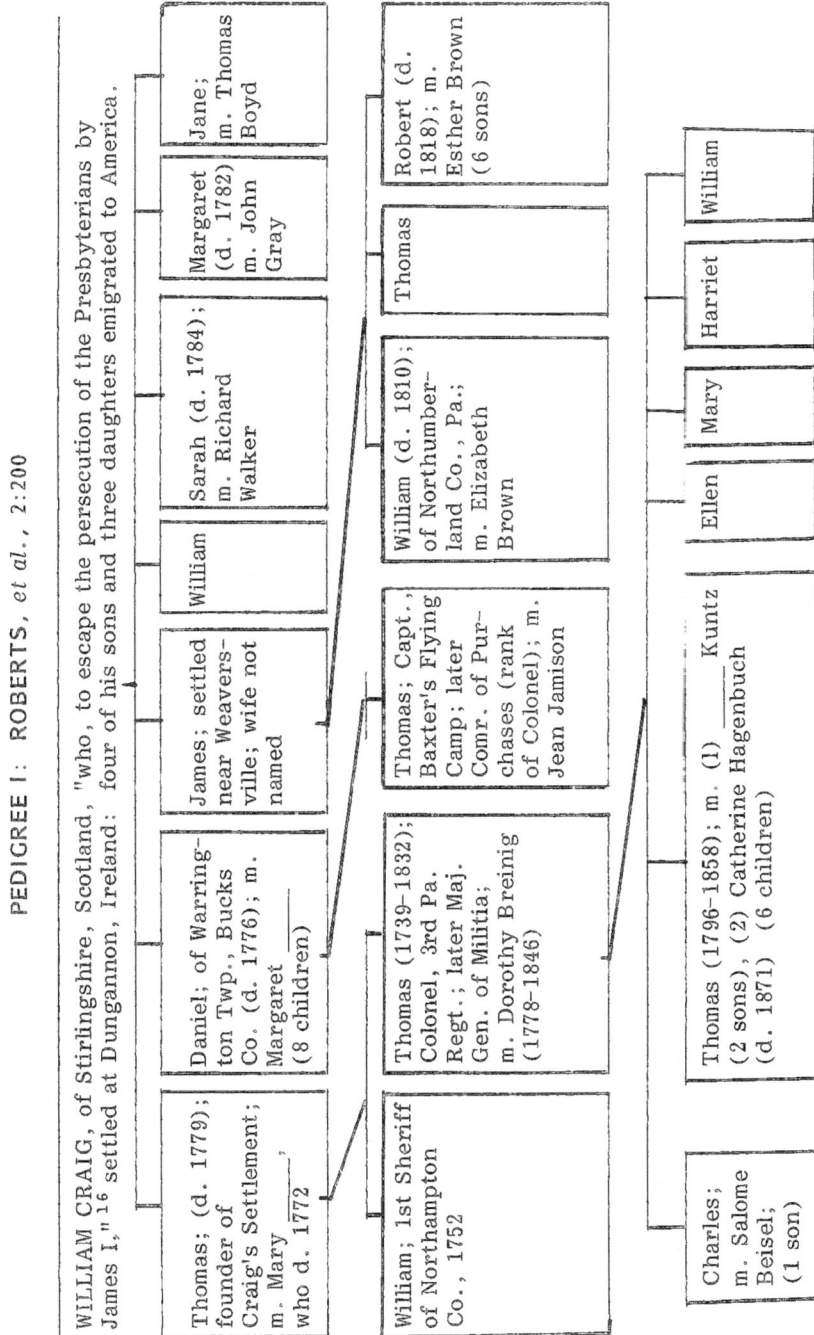

PEDIGREE II: ROBERTS, et al., 2:202

Colonel THOMAS CRAIG (no parentage shown); founder of Craig's Settlement, 1728; on roll of the Presbyterian Synod, Philadelphia, Pa.

Thomas Craig (1740-1832); Colonel, 3rd Pa. Regiment; Associate Judge, Montgomery Co., Pa., 1784-89; later of Stemblersville, Towamencing Twp., Northampton (now Carbon) Co.; Major General, 7th Division, Pennsylvania Militia; m. (1) _____ Kuntz, (2) Catherine Hagenbach (sic: Hagenbuch)

By 1st wife — Thomas; 4 years in House of Representatives; 3 in Senate

By 2nd wife:
- Eliza; m. Gen. Charles Heckman
- Allen; Dist. Judge at Mauch Chunk, Pa.
- William; in Nebraska
- Robert; Capt., U.S. Army

PEDIGREE III: CLEMENS, pp. 3-5

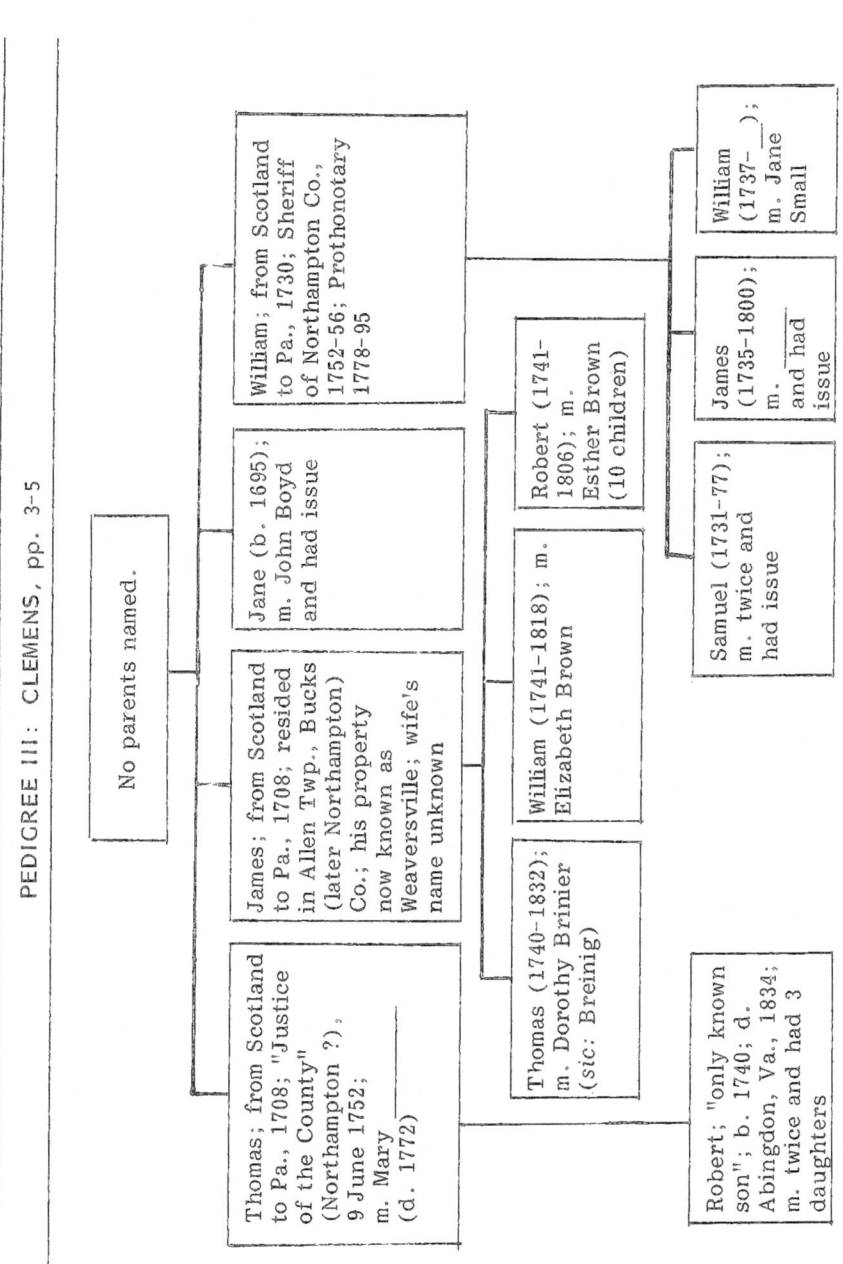

Although Roberts, *et al.*, two pedigrees differ in some respects, both agree that General Thomas Craig was a son of the Settlement's founder, Thomas Craig (who was *not* a colonel, at stated in Pedigree II). Clemens' pedigree claims that General Thomas's father was James, who is assigned (in all pedigrees) as Thomas the founder's brother. Clemens also telescopes two Williams into one, making him Sheriff in 1752-56 and Prothonotary in 1778-95.

Other accounts of the early Craigs are equally confusing. Until a few years ago no one apparently attempted to make a serious study of the Revolutionary generations of the family. And even now, in spite of all the documentation at hand, we cannot be sure of reconstructing all of the family relationships. Our plan is to present a series of sketches of individuals and family groups, insofar as they are shown by the records, and to determine, if possible, the correct pedigree.

## 4. THOMAS CRAIG, ESQ., OF ALLEN TOWNSHIP

Thomas Craig (born *ca.* 1695) is reputed to have been a son of a certain Scotsman, William Craig, who allegedly emigrated from Stirlingshire, Scotland, to Dungannon, Ireland. There is no proof of this paternity, but his father may very well have been named William. An article in *The Presbyterian* in 1847 suggested that Thomas may have come from Dublin. He is generally considered to be the founder of Craig's Settlement in Bucks (later Northampton) County. His arrival in the county is generally assigned to the year 1728.

Thomas's name is said[6] to occur in 1731 as the first elder of the Presbyterian congregation in Allen Township in the roll of the Philadelphia Synod, but it must be noted that Allen Township was not created until 11 June 1748.

Thomas Craig lived on a tract of 500 acres purchased from Caspar Wistar on 20 March 1739. Although he took an interested part in local affairs, he was not among the 37 residents of Bucks County who petitioned for the creation of Allen Township in 1748. He had been appointed Justice of the Peace in 1745, and on 9 June 1752 his appointment was renewed.[7] His son William was the first sheriff and his brother Daniel the first treasurer of Northampton County, under the Act of 11 March 1752 creating the county. This led to fears that a Craig dynasty was in control of the county. William Parsons, a Philadelphian now resident in Northampton County, in a letter to Benjamin Franklin, 15 January 1753 (quoted by Henry in his manuscript history of the county), was highly critical of the Craigs. He wrote that the sheriff's father, Thomas Craig, "is President of our Courts." This may be true, as it is a contemporary statement, but we have found nothing to confirm it.

The land transactions of Thomas Craig may be summarized as follows:

> 9 April 1753: Thomas Craig, of Allenstown, Co. of Northampton, Province of Pa., and Mary his wife, sold to James Barclay, of Warrington, Co. of Bucks, husbandman (who had

married his niece Margaret Craig), a tract of land in Warrington Twp. that had been purchased from Willian Allen, Esq., of Philadelphia and Margaret his wife. Neighboring landowners included Daniel Craig (his brother). Thomas signed; Mary made her mark. Recorded 1 April 1760.[8]

19 December 1753: Thomas Craig, Esq., of Allentown, etc., and Mary his wife mortgaged to William Logan, of Stenton, Northern Liberties of Philadelphia, a tract of 305 acres, part of 500 acres and 96 perches which he had obtained from Caspar Wister (sic)[21] by indenture, 28 March 1739. The debt for which this property was mortgaged was £254.02.02. Thomas signed, Mary made her mark, and witnesses were Nicholas Scull and Wm. Parsons.[22] Recorded 10 January 1754.[9]

4 February 1772: Thomas Craig, Esq., of Allen Twp., and Mary his wife mortgaged to William Logan, Esq., of Philadelphia, their plantation and tract of land in Morris Twp. (boundaries described; among adjoining landowners, James Craig) which had been granted by Caspar Wistar to Thomas Craig as previously reported. Recorded 7 February 1772.[10]

Mary Craig died on 14 July 1772, aged 75 years, and was buried in the Presbyterian Burial Ground, Scotch-Irish Settlement, near Weaversville, Northampton County, Pennsylvania. Thomas died between 25 November 1772, date of his Will, and 6 January 1779, date of its probate. His tombstone merely gives the year 1779 as date of death.[11]

In his Will "Thomas Craig of Allen Township in the County of Northampton in the Province of Pennsylvania, Senior," states that he is "very Aged & Infirm in Body, but of Sound Mind and Memory." He made the following provisions:

To my well-beloved cousin, Thomas Craig, Son of my Brother Daniel, £17.10.0. Current Money of the Province of Pennsylvania.

To my grandson, William Craig, £10.0.0., said currency, "besides his part that is hereafter mentioned."

And the better to enable my Executors to dispose of my real estate which I do order and will to be sold (with all my goods and chattels), I hereby give full power and authority unto my executors to bargain, sell and convey all my lands, tenements and hereditaments, etc., etc.

Immediately after my decease my Executors are to settle with Mr. William Logan, of the City of Philadelphia, all my concerns and dealings with him.

When my lands and other effects are sold, and my just debts paid, the "Remaining Neat" [net] amount to be divided into ten equal shares, as follows:

To Elizabeth Craig, my daughter-in-law, one-tenth part thereof; to my son William's children, each one-tenth part thereof: Thomas, Hugh, Charles, William, Mary, Sarah, Margaret, Elizabeth, and Ann.

My daughter-in-law, Elizabeth Craig, and all my grandchildren that shall be at age at my decease, shall receive their respective shares twelve months after my decease, and the minor children to be paid their respective shares, viz$^t$. the males at 21 and the females at 18.

Executors: My much-esteemed brother-in-law, Richard Walker, Esq., Arthur Lattimore, and John Ralston.

Witnesses: Will$^m$. Carruthers, Robert Lattimore, Thomas Herron.

Thomas Craig signed his Will by mark, an indication that he was in a very enfeebled condition, for the deed books of earlier years showed he had signed his name.

On 7 January 1779 John Hays and William Kerr made an inventory of Thomas Craig's "goods & chattles rights & credits." It was witnessed by two of the executors, Walker and Ralston. A summary follows:

"Wearing Apparell to wit one Coat three Jacets two shirts two pair of trousers one piece of Linen Cloath one Hat" (£16.0.0.); one trunk (£0.1.0.); two capes, one pair of mittons (£1,17.6.); two stocks, one silver stock _____ [illegible] (£3.0.0.); one armed chair (£1.2.6.); "one bed tick and fethers" (£22.1.0.); one bed quilt (£2.5.0.); one pair of double blankets (£7.10.0.); one sheet (£1.17.6.); one bolster & pillow (£2.5.0.); one pair of britches and one pair of stockings (£10.5.0.); one large Bible (£0.15.0.); one _____ [illegible] book (£0.15.0.); one pocket book (£0.5.0.); one old great coat (£1.2.6.); cash (£13.4.3.); loan office certificate of 500 dollars (£187.10.0.); one bond of seventy-three (£73.0.0.). Total: £336.19.3.

On 30 October 1779 "John Ralston, Esquire, the only acting Executor of the Last Will and Testament of Thomas Craig late of Allen Township in the County of Northampton Esquire," submitted his account of the settlement of Craig's estate. He charged himself with all goods, chattels, rights and credits of the deceased, as shown in the inventory (£336.9.3.). The said goods sold for more at public vendue than the appraised value (£26.7.9.), "With Interest received on money put into the Loan Office & a Bond of £73.0.0." (£366.0.6.). The total of these items was £729.7.6. He made cash payments and disbursements to several people as shown by their receipts: John Arndt, Register of Wills, for letters testamentary (£2.5.0.), Richard Walker (£26.0.0.), Rob$^t$. Lattimore, three different sums (£15.15.0., £18.17.0., £3.2.0.), Will$^m$. Congleton (£5.0.0.), Evan Davis (£0.5.0.), and "Patrick Stewart crying vendue" (£3.0.0.). He paid (£4.10.0. cash "for this Settlement & Copy." He allowed the accountant (himself) his commission for receiving £729.7.6. at 5% (£3.18.8.). Total: £40.8.0. The balance in the hands of the accountant amounted to

£610.5.6.[12]

The Craig genealogy published by Roberts, *et al.*, assigns two sons, William and Thomas (afterwards the general) to Thomas and Mary Craig. This is erroneous; Thomas mentions only one son in his will, although he leaves him no bequest, and he gives legacies to William's wife and children

We will discuss the son William, who probably predeceased his father, in the next section. For the moment let us consider Thomas's siblings (real and presumed). They are Daniel, James, William, Sarah, Margaret, and Jane. Daniel will be treated separately, also James, who, however, was described by the Rev. Richard Webster in 1847 as being unrelated to Thomas.[13] For the present Thomas's "brother" William must remain ephemeral; we cannot identify any of the William Craigs as this man.

Sarah Craig, Thomas's sister, was born *ca.* 1706. She married Richard Walker, who was born in 1702, the son of William and Ann Walker of Neshaminy, Bucks County, Pennsylvania. He was a prominent citizen, serving as a member of the Provincial Assembly from 1747 to 1759, and as a Justice of the Peace of the Bucks County Courts from 1749 to 1775. He was commissioned a captain in the Provincial Service, 12 February 1749. During the Revolutionary War he was a member of the Committee of Safety. He was a faithful Presbyterian, serving as an elder in the Neshaminy Church.[14]

Richard Walker was closely associated with the Craigs in a number of real estate transactions. On 15 June 1745 he joined with eight others, including David Craige, of Warrington Township, Bucks County, in purchasing two acres and ten perches of land on which to build a meeting house in Warwick Township. Among the eight sellers of the land were James Craig, of Warminster, Bucks County, yeoman, and Walker's brother-in-law, John Gray, of Warminster, yeoman, husband of Margaret Craig. They were described as members of the Protestant Congregation of Warwick and the adjacent townships of the denominations of Presbyterians.[15]

Over a period of years (1763-73) Richard Walker was involved with John Craig, of Warrington Township, innkeeper, in buying and selling land.

Sarah (Craig) Walker died on 24 April 1784, aged 78 years, and Richard died on 11 April 1791, aged 89 years. Both are buried at Neshaminy. They apparently had no children as Richard's estate was divided among the descendants of his brothers and sisters.[16]

Thomas Craig's other sister, Margaret, married John Gray, of Neshaminy, Bucks County, where he was an elder in the Presbyterian Church from 1743. His plantation was on the northwest side of the Bristol road, extending northwardly from the present village of Warrington. He and Margaret had four children: John, James, Mary, and Jean. The father died on 27 April 1749. In his Will he did not mention his sons, but gave small legacies to his nephews and nieces, then devised his whole estate to his wife Margaret for life, and finally, to his "Brother" Richard Walker and two clergymen in trust: £2 per annum to be paid for support of the ministry at Neshaminy, and one-half "for the benefit of Rev. Charles Beatty during his ministry at the new meeting house at Warwick." The other half was for one of the "Religious Students for the Ministry," when Beatty ceases to preach, whole of the profits thereof for the use of such students forever. Margaret (Craig) Gray survived her husband many years, dying between April 1782, when she made her Will, and March 1783, when it was probated. She said she was "far advanced in years." Her son, John Gray, settled in the Tuscarora Valley in the present Juniata County, near Fort Bingham. While he was away getting some provisions, the fort was attacked by Indians and his wife and daughter taken prisoner to Canada. The daughter was never heard from again, and after fruitless efforts to locate them, John died in 1759 leaving a Will providing for his wife and child if they should come back. The wife eventually escaped and returned to Bucks County. She, too, tried to get news of her daughter, but without success. She remarried eventually, but for some reason she failed to offer her first husband's will for probate until 1785; the long delay complicated the settlement of the estate of John Gray (Jr.) and a 50-year-long lawsuit ensued.[17]

We have no information about Thomas Craig's alleged third sister, Jane, and her husband, John Boyd.

## 5. WILLIAM CRAIG, SHERIFF OF NORTHAMPTON COUNTY

William Craig was the *only* son (in spite of other claims) of Thomas Craig, the founder of Craig's Settlement. It is estimated that he was born between 1715 and 1720. The Northampton County deed books reveal that at various times he acquired and disposed of large tracts of land on a branch of the Bushkill above the Forks of the Delaware, on the North Branch of the River Delaware, several other tracts above the Forks of the Delaware, two tracts beyond the Blue Mountain, etc.[18]

William Craig was Sheriff of Northampton County from 1752 to 1756. His actions and his plurality of offices caused considerable dissatisfaction. William Parsons, a member of Assembly who had gone to Northampton County from Philadelphia, in the letter to Benjamin Franklin, 15 January 1753 (mentioned in our account of Thomas Craig), had some unflattering things to say about the Craigs: "I must confess that if you were not a Member of the Honourable House I should hardly have troubled you now about the Situation of any of the publick Affairs of this County. Some of which are the Occasion of uneasiness to some of the Inhabitants. And amongst other Things the great power of the Sherif which with us is at present something extraordinary. As he is not only Sherrif: but Treasurer of the County and Clerk to the Commissioners and Assessors. His father is president of our Court, his Wife's Father [Hugh Wilson] and several of his very intimate Friends make up almost our whole Bench of Justices. And some of these with a Jury of his own summoning are the Persons who are to adjust and allow all his accounts with the publick. . . The Power of Sherrif is almost exorbitant as he is the sole judge of Elections and himself a Candidate. And has it wholly in his own power to summons who he pleases for Jurymen. And our Sherif besides all this acts publickly as a Justice of the Peace for this County by virtue of a Commission of the Peace granted before his Sheriffalty and how far that is agreeable to Law others may determine it. People with us think it shows a strong desire after Dominion. . ."[19]

At about the time this letter was written the General Assembly received four petitions from inhabitants of Northampton County who lodged the same complaints against Sheriff Craig that Parsons described. They declared that if the offices held by him were "vested in several Persons," they would, "as the Petitioners Conceive, be likely to be better discharge as they would probably be a Check upon each other. . ." They charged further that "he has of late gone from one Tavern to another, throughout a great part of the said County, issuing his Precepts to bring Persons before him, and there hearing and determining Actions for small Debts, and giving public Notice, from Time to Time, at what Tavern he will next attend, whereby great Numbers of People, some of them very disorderly, are drawn together, and being many of them heated and intoxicated with Liquor, have been induced to put their Neighbors in Trouble and Expense for very trivial Matters. . ."[20]

The case dragged on for several months, with charges and counter-charge being exchanged between Craig and his accusers. Finally, after first ignoring an order to appear before the Assembly's Committee of Grievance the sheriff went to Philadelphia where further inquiry was made into his conduct, and he faced personally one of his Northampton County critics, Assessor John Jones. On 28 August 1753 he was called on the carpet and severely reprimanded, "and, acknowledging his Fault, and promising to behave in such a Manner as to give no cause of Complaint in the future, he was dismissed."[21]

William Craig was commissioned a captain in the provincial Militia by Governor James Hamilton in December, 1755.[22] It is amusing that his immediate superior was the man who had so severely criticized his conduct as sheriff Major William Parsons. Parsons was loyal to the proprietary government, and placing the frontier companies under his command reflected the suspicion directed against many of the frontier officers. A letter written by Richard Peters to the Proprietor, Thomas Penn, on 17 February 1756, declared that the frontiersmen commissioned by Hamilton were "generally men of no character, and elected on their own solicitation by some of the meanest of their Neighbours, and this done too in hopes of their being taken into pay."[23] The patriotism was rather questionable; a delegation from the Irish Settlement, led by Hugh Wilson and Thomas Craig (father-in-law and father of our captain) went to Franklin, "and demanded an Addition of 30 Men to Craig's Company, or threatened they would immediately one and all leave their Country to the Enemy."[24]

There is extant a letter, 10 February 1756, from Captain William Craig to Timothy Horsfield, commanding officer at Bethlehem, who had ordered him to escort some wagons with provisions to Fort Allen. "I am heartily willing to do everything in my power consistent with the trust reposed in me," he wrote, "but sundry of my men being sick at present, it will be very difficult for me to march all my men out of the settlement, besides the people of the settlement are extremely uneasy at my leaving them without a proper guard, and my whole Company as to numbers is not too many upon such an occasion. However as the common cause requires it, I am willing, and will hold myself ready accordingly, only I would desire the favor of you to send no waggons but such as are strong and able, being much fatigued with some of the last."[25] Craig and his 41-man company were at Fort Hamilton, near the present Stroudsburg, Monroe County (as it became later), 23 February 1756,[26] and on 15 March 1756 he was paid £256.13.3. for himself and his company.[27] This seems to be the last record of his military service.

William Craig died sometime between 4 March 1766, when, for £120, he bought a tract of land in Northampton County from Peter Fox, of Allen Township, and 25 November 1772, when his father, Thomas, made his Will. Considering his prominence, it is strange that he apparently made no Will, and we can find no probate of his estate.

We know from his father's will that his wife was named Elizabeth. According to the Rev. Mr. Webster, writing in 1847, she was daughter of Hugh Wilson, one of the leaders of the Craig Settlement, and prominent in provincial affairs. Wilson died intestate before 25 May 1774, when his oldest son Thomas, of Allen Township, renounced administration of the estate in favor of his brother, Samuel Wilson.

Elizabeth Craig, William's widow, engaged in the following land transactions:

    10 August 1773: Deed from Andrew Hagenbach [Hagenbuch] of \_\_\_\_, Bucks Co., Pa., yeoman, and Margaret his wife, to Elizabeth Craig of Allen Twp., Northampton Co., widow. Consideration: £5. A certain lot or piece of ground in Allen Twp.: one acre of land, part or parcel of a certain large tract of land (500 acres and 96 perches) which the Proprietaries had granted to Caspar Wister of the City of Philadelphia on 25 November 1738, and which said Wister and Catherine his wife on 28 March 1739 had sold to Thomas Craig, Esq., of Bucks Co. The said Thomas by indenture, 28 June 1773, had granted to Hagenbach, his heirs and assigns, 155 acres of the aforesaid land, and this one acre was part of the aforesaid 155 acres. Witnesses: James Taylor, Jn$^o$. Jennings. Recorded 27 May 1774.[29]

    24 August 1773 William Allen, of the City of Philadelphia, to Elizabeth Craig, widow, of Allen's Twp., Northampton Co. Consideration: £20. A certain tract of land or piece of land in Allen's Twp.: 5 acres. Recorded 28 May 1774.[30]

    4 June 1799: Elizabeth Craig, widow, of Allen Twp., Northampton Co. To Ann Taylor, of same place, widow of James Taylor, deceased. Plantation and two tracts or parcels of land in Allen Twp. (1) Boundaries described: lands late of William Craig, Andrew Hagenbach, Elizabeth Craig. Same premises which William Allen granted to Elizabeth Craig on 24 August 1773. (2) Boundaries described: lands of Andrew Hagenbuch and late of William Craig. 100 acres and two perches, part of 500 acres and 96 perches which the Proprietaries by patent of 25 November 1738 granted to Caspar Wistar of Philadelphia, and said Wistar and Catherine his wife on 8 March 1739 granted to Thomas Craig, of Bucks Co., etc. Said Thomas Craig on 28 June 1773 granted to Andrew Hagenbuch and his heirs and assigns 155 acres of this tract. On 10 August 1773 Hagenbuch granted one acre to Elizabeth Craig.[31]

Thomas Craig's 1772 Will named his son William's nine children: Thomas, Hugh, Charles, William, Mary, Sarah, Margaret, Elizabeth, and Ann. The last-named daughter was the widow of James Taylor to whom her mother conveyed land in 1799. As evidence of this family connection in Elizabeth' deeds the name of William's father, Thomas, and the property he acquired from Caspar Wistar keep cropping up. Moreover, in Ann Taylor's estate papers her administrator, General Thomas Craig, is described as her *brother,* and the Rev. Mr. Webster wrote of this family in 1847: "Thomas Craig is said to have come from Dublin, an upright, pious man; the stone he erected to his wife is the only one in the graveyard. *His only son, William, married a daughter of Hugh Wilson; one of his sons was General Thomas Craig; another son, Hugh, died young, when about to prepare for the ministry.*" (Italics ours.)

## 6. GENERAL THOMAS CRAIG

Thomas Craig, the eldest son of William and Elizabeth (Wilson) Craig, was born about 26 October 1739.[32]

His first public appearance was in 1769 when he was a member of the Northampton County Grand Jury to hear the case against 30 men accused of "riotously routously tumultuously and unlawfully" gathering together with force of arms "with an Intention the Peace of our said Lord the King to disturb." They disturbed the peace by invading the property of the Proprietors of Pennsylvania, Thomas and Richard Penn, and causing great damage.[33]

This was the time of the Yankee-Pennamite wars when the colony of Connecticut claimed the upper-third of Pennsylvania and, beginning in 1753, threw settlers into the northeastern counties of the Penns' province. So many of these swarmed into the Wyoming Valley in present Luzerne County, that troops from Northampton and other counties were hastily raised to march against the invaders and to attempt to drive them out. Thomas Craig participated in this expedition, led by Northampton County Sheriff John Jennings. He is recorded as having conducted himself with great heroism.[34] Toward the end of 1769 Jennings recorded a payment of £6.18.6. "To Thomas Craig got Sumoning men & goeing to Wioming, his time & Expences."[35]

Like all Scotch-Irish settlers Thomas Craig was always spoiling for a fight, and when the Revolutionary War broke out he was ready. He volunteered for service on the advice of Mr. John Allen, who gave him a letter of recommendation to Colonel William Thompson, then commanding a regiment of Pennsylvania riflemen. He was commissioned Third Lieutenant on 25 June 1775, and went with Thompson to Cambridge, Massachusetts. He was raised to Second Lieutenant, 8 November 1775. On 5 January 1776 he was commissioned a Captain in the Second Pennsylvania Battalion (afterwards redesignated the Third Pennsylvania Regiment), commanded by Colonel Arthur St. Clair, and immediately marched to Canada, taking part in the abortive invasion of the British colony.

Craig was skipped over the rank of Major and promoted to Lieutenant

Colonel in January 1777, to rank from 9 September 1776. In June 1777 the regiment joined the main army at Morristown, New Jersey, and on 1 August 1777 Craig was commissioned Colonel, succeeding Colonel Joseph Wood as regimental commander, a position he held until the end of the war. He participated in the battles of Short Hills, Brandywine, Germantown, and Monmouth. He was at Valley Forge during the dreadful winter of 1777-78 and was President of Courts Martial held in January and February 1778.[36] He was one of three officers appointed to superintend military hospitals in Pennsylvania.[37] In February 1779 Caleb Brokaw, a New Jersey citizen, complained to General Washington that Colonel Craig had beaten and "otherwise ill-treated" him. The Commander-in-Chief appointed a Court of Inquiry to look into the matter and report to him. The officers comprising the Court reached the conclusion that since the inhabitants of a state did not consider themselves as being under military jurisdiction any complaints they had against officers and soldiers should be referred to a civil court. This aroused the General's ire, and in a scathing reply he sternly recommended "to all officers to consider the delicacy of their situation with respect to the Inhabitants and cautiously to refrain from every thing that may even have the appearance of an abuse of power."[38]

Colonel Craig marched south in the fall of 1781 and was present at the surrender of Lord Cornwallis at Yorktown, 19 October 1781. He arrived too late to participate in the siege, as shown by Colonel Richard Butler's letter to General William Irvine, 22 October 1781: "Col. Craig & his detach't arrived just in time for some of his officers to see the surrender."[39]

Craig and his troops went to South Carolina some time after the events at Yorktown. From there, in March 1782, they took the long trail home, and Craig retired from the service 1 January 1783. On Tuesday, 30 September 1783, the Continental Congress "*Resolved*, That the Secretary of War issue to all officers in the army, under the rank of major general, who hold the same rank now that they held in 1777, a brevet commission, one grade higher than their present rank, having respect to their present seniority . . ."[40] It is not certain if this applied to recently retired officers; Craig does not appear in later records as Brevet Brigadier General, and as late as 1785 he is still referred to in the journals of Congress as Colonel Craig.[41] Following the war he engaged in many land transactions, in not one of which was he given a military title; he was regularly mentioned as Thomas Craig, Esq., until he obtained a major general's commission in the Pennsylvania militia; thereafter, he was regularly described as General Thomas Craig.[42]

The journals of Congress have the following record, 18 October 1783: "The Committee of the week report that the petition of Thomas Craig late Colo. of the 3rd Pennsylvania Regiment and others setting forth that they were deranged and incurred a considerable expence in a journey of 800 miles and praying an allowance therefor be referred to the Secretary of War to report."[43] Apparently the Secretary's report was favorable, for on 16 April 1784 Congress directed him to issue warrants on the Paymaster General in favor of Colonel Craig and the other officers to pay them $30 as an extra allowance to defray their traveling expenses.[44]

Craig was issued Bounty Land Warrant No. 409-500 on 27 February 1792, for his war services. There are no papers about the land in his pension file, so we do not know where it was located.

During the early part of the war Craig had transferred his residence from Northampton County to Norristown, Philadelphia (now Montgomery) County, for on 1 April 1777 Thomas Craig, describing himself as "of Norristown," purchased for five shillings from John Kline, of Towamensing Township, Northampton County, and Juliana his wife, a certain messuage and tenement and plantation or tract of land of 108 acres in Towamensing. The deed was recorded 10 April 1777.[45] He owned real estate in both Northampton and Montgomery Counties. The indentures whereby he bought and sold land were so numerous that to recite them would be tedious.

Montgomery County was formed from Philadelphia by an Act of the General Assembly, 10 September 1784. On the same day he was appointed the new county's first Associate Judge and Prothonotary (Clerk of the Court of Common Pleas). The next year (1785) he became Recorder of Deeds. He held these offices until 1789. Shortly thereafter, he moved back to Northampton County.[46]

Thomas Craig's interest in military matters was continued after the war, when he became Lieutenant of Northampton County (commanding the county militia). On Sunday, 13 April 1793, Governor Thomas Mifflin appointed him Major General of the Second Division, composed of the Bucks and Montgomery counties militia. His commission was renewed by later governors; during the War of 1812 he commanded the Eighth Division.[47]

In 1792 Congress passed an Act providing pensions for officers and soldiers who were disabled in service. These were the only pensions until the Act of 18 March 1818, which covered officers and enlisted men of the Continental Establishment who were in "reduced circumstances." By this time General Craig had apparently suffered financial reverses. He applied for a pension on 20 April 1818. He forwarded to the Pension Office his commission as evidence of his service. He was inscribed on the Pension Roll of Pennsylvania at $20 a month, to commence as of 20 April 1818.

On 1 May 1820 Congress required all pensioners then on the rolls to file a schedule of property in their possession. General Craig did not get around to submitting his schedule until 28 January 1822. He reported that he owned eleven acres in Towamensing Township in the Blue Mountain. He had purchased an unpatented right to 61 acres, also in the Blue Mountain. He produced an "exemplification" (transcript) of a deed poll to his daughter Eliza, wife of Daniel Kraemer, with whom he was then living in the Borough of Northampton, Lehigh County.[48] In consideration of his natural love and affection for his daughter and also for $1 paid to him (to make the transaction legal) he granted to Eliza a messuage or tenement and two contiguous tracts of land in Lehigh or Towamensing Township in Northampton County. He gave these tracts to his daughter in gratitude for her care and attention during his recent illness.

His schedule included bonds against Charles Craig and Thomas Craig, Jr., (his sons), totalling $1,100. He wrote that he had many demands for £20,000 or £30,000[49] which he was confident he could never recover. He received a pension from the State of Pennsylvania of $180. payable semi-annually. He owed about £150. His household furniture was valued at

$200.

Although many pensioners lost their pensions because their schedules showed they were not as indigent as they had represented themselves to be, there is nothing in General Craig's file to show that he suffered the same fate.

General Craig returned to Northampton County to pass his last days. *The Northampton Whig*, of Easton, reported on Tuesday, 24 January 1832: "DIED—Gone! Departed this life, on Friday evening last [20 January] in this borough, Maj. Gen. Thomas Craig, aged 92 years, 1 month, 17 days..."[50] The paper gives a long account of his funeral services on Sunday, 22 January, which, characteristically, he had planned himself. It was a military funeral, with marching troops, ringing of bells, thunder of cannon, and an impressive sermon by the *Lutheran* clergyman, the Rev. Mr. Yeager.[51]

The paper eulogized him as follows: "In his character were combined the qualities of the soldier and the gentleman. He was strict in his soldier's discipline, yet generous and affable in his manners, and easy of approach when the time and occasion approved it. In the hour of danger he was brave, quick to conceive and prompt to execute. He possessed an active and intelligent mind, which faithfully served him to the last —— and although the infirmities of age compelled him to spend many of his last years in retirement, yet he was a cordial receiver of visitants. He delighted to speak of his military career and the triumph of his country's arms, at a time when his country was his idol, and its enemies his bitterest foes."

The paper failed to add that he had certain strong convictions from which nothing could shake him. During the Revolution he belonged to the Gates or anti-Washington faction. General Horatio Gates commanded the army during the unsuccessful invasion of Canada, in which Craig had participated. In 1777-78 there was a "cabal" to replace General Washington with Gates, and Craig was one of the officers who favored this action, which was never put into effect. But to the end of his life Craig never had a kind word for Washington, whose military qualities he disparaged. The other strong opinion he held was his vehement denial of the divinity of the Founder of the Christian faith.[52]

Charles Miner, in his history of Pennsylvania's Wyoming Valley, thus describes him: "Though brave as either, in his social walks he resembled Mark Antony rather than Scipio. Having quit the tented field, he sought excitement and pleasure, amid the lilies and the roses, with the blond and brunette beauties of the stream and hill, in old Northampton. Colonel (*sic*) Craig lived to the very advanced age of 93 (*sic*) years, having departed this life in January, 1832."[53]

General Craig is said to have married (date unknown) Dorothy Breinig (sometimes given as Brinier), who, according to the published genealogies, was born in 1778. *If true,* she was about 38 years younger than her husband. She died on 1 September 1846, and was buried at Lower Towamensing Church. They had six children: Charles, who married Salome Beisel, and had a son Benjamin; Thomas (1796-1858), hotel owner at Lehigh Water

Gap, and captain of a troop of horse in the Pennsylvania militia, who married Catherine Hagenbuch; Eliza, wife of Daniel Kraemer; Mary; Harriet (also called Henrietta?),[54] died on 1 October 1822; and William.

## 7. HUGH CRAIG

Hugh Craig was the second son of Sheriff William and Elizabeth (Wilson) Craig, according to the order of children in his grandfather Thomas Craig's Will. Heitman's *Historical Register* says of a Hugh Craig of Pennsylvania: "Paymaster, 11th Pennsylvania, 4 December 1776; resigned 31st January, 1777." This is at variance with a "Return of the 11 Pen. Regiment Rich$^d$. Humpton Colonel —— Raised 27$^{th}$ Sep$^t$ 1776 and incorporated with the 10$^{th}$ Pens. Regiment 24$^{th}$ June 1778," dated at White Plains, 30 August 1778; "Craige [no first name given] Paymaster. Never joyned the Reg$^t$. And$^w$. Eppler appointed Pay Master 14 Aprl 1777. Resigned 1 March 1778."[55] What record Heitman saw to tie *Hugh* Craig with the paymaster Craige who never reported for duty is unknown. However, our Hugh Craig had a short life. The Rev. Richard Webster, quoted above, wrote in 1847 that William Craig's son Hugh "died young, when about to prepare for the ministry."

## 8. CAPTAIN CHARLES CRAIG

Charles Craig was the third son of Sheriff William and Elizabeth (Wilson) Craig, as shown in his grandfather's Will. We believe he was the army officer, Captain Charles Craig, in Heitman's *Historical Register*. General Thomas Craig, when applying for a pension in 1818 and reciting his military service, said that he volunteered on the advice of Mr. John Allen, who gave him a letter of recommendation to Colonel William Thompson. That letter also included Charles, as shown by the following letter from Colonel Thompson, 14 November 1775:[56]

> "Your friends, the two Mr. Craigs, whom you mentioned in your letter to me before my Reg$^t$. marched, have behaved in such a manner, during the Campaign, as to merit every Friendship in my power to confer on them; and Fortune has in some measure put it in my way to serve them. Captain Miller got tired of the Service & Regiment, and Charles being by the Committee of that County appointed first Lieu$^t$. has got the Company."

Charles Craig was commissioned First Lieutenant in Captain Abraham Miller's Company, Thompson's Pennsylvania Rifle Regiment, 25 June 1775, and was appointed to Captain 9 November 1775. He served with the First Continental Infantry from 1 January to 31 December 1776. The following record appears in the journals of Congress, Tuesday, 13 May 1777:[57]

> "Resolved, That 800 dollars be advanced to Captain Craig, of the light horse, for the use of his troop; he to be accountable.

> "*Ordered*, That the Board of War enquire into the
> truth of a report that Captain Craig has inlisted into his
> troop some deserters and prisoners of the enemy, and
> take such measures as are consistent with the resolutions
> of Congress and the public service."

The Board reported "that they have enquired into the situation of Captain Craig's troop, and find there are no deserters from the enemy or prisoners of war."[58]

Craig became a Captain in the Fourth Continental Dragoons, commanded by Colonel Stephen Moylan, 10 July 1777. Heitman says he was "wounded at Brandywine, 11th September, 1777, and did not rejoin the army." He may have been wounded, but he continued to serve in the army, as shown in Washington's General Orders of 9 November 1777, as follows:

> "Captain Craig of Moylan's regt., with his party of
> horse, has taken seven British dragoons, and seven
> soldiers, with their horses, arms and ammunition. The
> General desires Captain Craig, Capt. Lee, and the other
> officers who have distinguished themselves will accept his
> cordial thanks for the enterprise, spirit and bravery they
> have exhibited in harassing and make captives of the
> enemy."[59]

Philadelphia was occupied by the British from 26 September 1777 to 18 June 1778. There is a tradition, reported by Watson, the annalist, based on "very direct and certain evidence," that Lydia Darrach, wife of a Philadelphia teacher, overheard the British adjutant general, who was quartered at her house, discussing plans for attacking the American army. On the pretext of going to Frankford for flour for family use, she slipped out of the house and headed to where the American army lay. On the way (where, is not stated, but presumably outside the city limits, for she had a pass to go through the lines), she met Captain Craig and reported the conversation to him. He "immediately rode off to General Washington, to put him on his guard. The next night, about midnight, the British army in great force marched silently[60] out of Philadelphia. The whole affair terminated in what was called, I believe, the action of Edgehill, on the 5th of Dec.; and on the 8th following, the British got back to the city, fatigued and disappointed."[61]

This story may be apocryphal: Watson does not cite his "very direct and certain evidence." As he died in 1860 he may very well have heard it as a young man, perhaps from Mrs. Darrach herself.

Charles Craig is named in a Bicentennial publication as one of the "intelligence officers who served with distinction during the war of independence."[62]

In December 1777 and the early months of 1778, Captain Craig's loyalty was questioned. He was seen lurking near the British lines and talking to William Allen and Abel James, who came out from Philadelphia to see him. One unidentified informant said, "Cap$^{tn}$ Crage" was "there (*sic*) spie (*sic*) ever since the[y] [the British] came to town." In a deposition sworn to at

York Town (York, Pennsylvania) before General Horatio Gates, President of the Board of War, 11 March 1778, Abraham Wilt declared:

"... the widow Waggoner of Kensington was at my father's house in Second Street, Philadelphia, where I heard her say, that a few days before, she saw capt: Craig of the light dragoons, the same who had been stationed on the Frankford road, dismount his horse near the enemy's lines to lead him a little way till he met Abel James & Colo. William Allen[63] with whom he shook hands, that after some conversation he led his horse a little way back, then mounted & rode off; and James and Allen turned towards the city; that no person accompanied Capt. Craig to this interview; and that she saw him at several other times riding towards town alone, but not so low down as when he met James & Allen; and that she said she was ready to be qualified in this her declaration... I have often heard the citizens say it was reported among the British Officers capt. Craig was of more service to the British troops than if he was with them in the city. The citizens conjectured he was thus serviceable by communicating intelligence of Gen$^l$. Washington's army."[64]

We have no way of knowing the truth of these accusations. Apparently the case was never tried before a Court Martial, so Craig's side of the story is not known. At any rate, he was annoyed and uneasy enough to send Washington the following letter, from Reading, Berks County, Pennsylvania, 5 March 1778.[65]

"I beg leave to inform your Excellency that the situation of my Private Affairs obliges me to request permission to quit the service.

"That is the Motive, Sir, which is my principal inducement to resigning; but there are several additional Reasons that render my continuance in the Army impracticable — the Promotion of Major Washington who was my inferior in point of rank. I cannot view in any other Light than as an oblique Reflection upon my Character as an officer, and I should at this time have applied for Liberty to resign had not my attachment to the cause and a regard for my own Honor induced me to suspend it Till the close of the Campaign.

"In justice to my reputation I must likewise observe that many insinuations were thrown out at Head Quarters respecting my conduct at the Lines, which were extremely unjust and malicious. And it gave me great Pain to find that they appeared to have some Weight with your Excellency. These are circumstances, Sir, which must disturb any Man of Sentiment and I presume your Excellency would not require any other Reasons for my Wish to leave the Army were they the only ones I had to adduce."

This letter was written in Reading, where at an unspecified time he married

Charlotte Bird. Her father, Mark Bird, was a well-to-do owner of an iron works at Birdsboro, on the Schuylkill, about nine miles below Reading. His sister, Rachel Bird, was wife of James Wilson, a signer of the Declaration of Independence. Mark's second wife was the mother of Charlotte (Bird) Craig, Catherine Van Gezel. One of her sisters, Gertrude, had married George Read, a signer of the Declaration of Independence, and another sister, Catherine, was the wife of Brigadier General William Thompson (the Craigs' friend and former commander of the 3rd Pennasylvania Regiment). By his wife, Charlotte, Captain Craig had a son, Charles.[66]

He was apparently not happy in his marriage. His friend, Charles Biddle, of Philadelphia, who knew most of the Craigs, relates that "he left the army at the request of Mark Bird, of Reading, and married his daughter. After the marriage he wanted Craig to retract something he had said about him. This Craig did not think, as a man of honor, he could do. On his refusing, Bird did everything in his power to injure him. Craig declared several times to me, before I left Reading that Bird had used him so ill that he had a great mind to shoot him. Having spent all his money, and being bred to no business, he thought if he were gone Bird would take home his wife and child. He therefore determined to put an end to his own existence..."[67]

Captain Craig's suicide, on 12 July 1782, created a sensation and was reported in diaries and journals that were later published, and in Charles Biddle's autobiography. But an account, written on the day of the occurrence, is contained in a letter from Daniel Brodhead, Jr., of Reading, to Walter Jenifer Stone, of Charles County, Maryland:[68]

> "...After taking such precautions as were requisite to prevent Detection, he laid himself on the Bed, raising his head, with several Pillows, to a convenient Height; he placed the muzzle of the Pistol under one Ear, and discharged its Contents, which went quite thro' his Head. The report of the Pistol brought up his Brother Colonel Thos. Craig, who immediately burst open the door (he having had the Precaution to bolt it on the inner Side) but the unfortunate Charles was already quite dead.--- I ought here to take Notice, that, least (sic) the Pistol should by any Means have proved ineffectual, he had provided his Sword, which lay across his Breast when his Brother entered the Room, so determined was he on the Perpetration of this shocking Deed."

Captain Craig left no Will. His estate was administered by his brother, Captain William Craig. The inventory of his personal estate listed a silver watch, a silver mounted fowling piece, a silver mounted sword, and a mulatto slave.

## 9. CAPTAIN WILLIAM CRAIG

William Craig was the fourth son of Sheriff William and Elizabeth (Wilson) Craig, according to the Will of grandfather Thomas Craig.

He was commissioned Ensign in Captain John Huling's Company, Second Pennsylvania Battalion, 5 January 1776. He was promoted to Second Lieutenant, Third Pennsylvania Regiment, 11 November 1776, and First Lieutenant, 1 January 1777. He was commissioned Captain, 4 July 1777, and served until his resignation on 1 June 1779.

Captain Craig's later life is obscure. We know only that he administered the estate of his deceased brother Charles in 1782. We had thought he might have been the William Craig, Esq., who, beginning 1788 and later, held the offices of Prothonotary of Northampton County, Justice of the Peace for the District of the Town of Easton, Justice of the Court of Common Pleas, and Clerk of the Court of Quarter Sessions and Jail Delivery.[69] If Captain Craig had held all of these positions, surely some mention would have been made in the autobiography of the family friend, Charles Biddle. Instead, he paints a gloomy picture: "I went into a carriage into which they were obliged to lift me, and to walk the horses. I had in the carriage with me Capt. William Craig, brother to my late unfortunate friend, Charles Craig. He was a very stout young man and could carry me with ease in his arms. Poor William soon after fell a sacrifice to his intemperance. He was the person who sat up with me the first night after I had broken my knee. Poor fellow, I have lived to see him buried."[70] Egle's *Pennsylvania Genealogies* states that William was still living in May 1787, and died shortly thereafter. Apparently he was unmarried.


## 10. DANIEL CRAIG, OF WARRINGTON TWP., BUCKS CO., PA.

The evidence that Daniel Craig of Bucks County was the brother of Thomas Craig, founder of Craig's Settlement, and father of the foregoing Revolutionary War officers, is contained in the latter's Will in which he left a bequest to Thomas Craig, "son of my brother Daniel."

Daniel Craig was an early settler in Allen Township when that area was still in Bucks County. On 4 August 1736 he purchased for "five shillings lawful money of Pennsylvania" from William Allen, of Philadelphia, Esquire, and his wife Margaret two tracts of land in Warrington Township, one of 213 acres and 20 perches, the other of 31 acres. The deed was not recorded until 31 March 1783.[71]

From 1752 to 1753 he was Treasurer of Northampton County,[72] and by the Act of 11 March 1752 setting up the county, he was appointed Collector of the Excise of Spirituous Liquors.

Most of Daniel's life was spent placidly on his farm in Warrington Township, away from the turmoil of politics in Northampton County. He married Margaret Brumfield, as shown by a deed executed in August 1763: Daniel Craig, of Warrington Township, Bucks County, yeoman, and Margaret his wife, joined with Charles Stewart, of Plumstead Township, and William Scott, of Warwick Township, in selling real and personal effects to Robert Scott, of Warwick Township. The recital traced the descent of the land to Henry Jameson and John Stewart, who made partition and division of the land. John Stewart, by his Will of 13 January 1761 "Did thereby Constitute and appoint Margaret Brumfield (the Wife to the above-named Daniel Craig), Charles Stewart together with William Scott full executors with authority to sell and dispose of his real and Personal Estate. . ."[73]

On 26 July 1775, Daniel Craig of Warrington Township, Bucks County, Pennsylvania, made his Will. After stating that he was "far advanced in years, and commending his soul and body to be decently interred, and ordering his just debts and funeral expenses to be paid, he got down to business:

> To my dear and loving wife Margaret £100 lawful money of Pennsilvania (sic): 1 mare worth £15; 1 cow worth £5; all my household furniture; sum of £9 to be paid to her yearly for life, the first payment to be made one year after my decease; my residuary devisee and legatee to provide my wife with sufficient house-room in the dwelling house of him my said residuary devisee and legatee together with firewood and the keeping of a cow summer and winter during the natural life of her the said Margaret free of any cases or charges and what I have given her my said wife Margaret shall be in "lue" and full satisfaction of her dower or two thirds of my estate.
>
> To my son John Craig, £50.
>
> To my son William Craig, £10 over and besides the yearly interest of £150 to be paid by my residuary devisee and legatee either in cash or victuals as my executors shall deem meet, during the term of his natural life. After his death the said sum of £150 is to be paid equally between Mary, Sarah, Hugh, and Daniel, children of my said son William part or share of said child shall go to survivor or survisors.
>
> To my daughter Mary, wife of James Barckley, £20.
>
> To my daughter Sarah, wife of John Barnhill, £20.
>
> To my daughter Jane, wife of Samuel Barnhill, £20.
>
> To my daughter Mary Lewin, £5.
>
> To my daughter Rebecca, wife of Hugh Stephenson, £20.
>
> Aforesaid legacies to be paid at end of one year, and after the expiration of the lease that may be on my plantation at the time of my death.
>
> To my son Thomas Craig, all my plantation situated in Warrington Township now in the tenure and occupation of

William Robinson, Jun$^r$. together with the buildings, improvements and appurtenances thereunto belonging and also the rest and residue of my estate, both real and personal.

Executors: My brother-in-law, Richard Walker, Esq., and my son, Thomas Craig;

Witnesses: Tho. Lust, W$^m$. Bean, John Rickey. The witnesses stated that the testator having been blind for several years, guided his hand to the proper place "where he willingly made his mark to the Seal of this Will."

Proved 22 April 1777.[74]

Sarah Craig, one of Daniel's daughters, and her husband, John Barnhill, had a son Robert, who married Elizabeth Potts. Their daughter, Margaret Barnhill, married Cornelius Van Schaick Roosevelt, of New York, and had a son, Theodore, who married Martha Bulloch. They had two sons, Theodore, 26th President of the United States, and Elliott, father of Anna Eleanor Roosevelt, wife of her fifth cousin, Franklin Delano Roosevelt, the 32nd President.

## 11. COLONEL THOMAS CRAIG

Thomas Craig, the eldest son of Daniel and Margaret (Brumfield) Craig, was born on 27 February 1739 (1739/40?).[75] When the war broke out he joined a company of Associators of Warrington Township, Bucks County, and appears on their roll, 19 August 1775.[76] Prior to the passage of the Militia Act of 1777 Pennsylvanians organized fifty-three battalions of military "Associators," volunteers who served with the Pennsylvania Line of the Continental Army from 1775 to 1777.[77] In 1776 Thomas Craig was appointed a Captain in Colonel William Baxter's Battalion of the Flying Camp, and was captured at Fort Washington, 16 November 1776.[78] There is no record showing when he was released or exchanged. Heitman's *Historical Register* shows a Thomas Craig of Pennsylvania who was Quartermaster of the Ninth Pennsylvania Regiment from 1 January 1777 until his resignation in the following September. There is no evidence to show that this man is Thomas Craig of Bucks County, though, of course, he could have been. In 1780 our Thomas was appointed Commissary of Purchases in Bucks County, a position which carried the rank of Colonel — hence, the confusion between the two Colonels Craig.[79]

Thomas Craig passed the years after the war on his farm in Warrington Township. He did not use his military title, but is shown in the numerous deeds executed by him simply as Thomas Craig, yeoman. On 18 November 1759, he married Jane, daughter of Henry and Mary Jamison. He made his Will on 29 February 1812 (proved 8 May 1813) and died on 22 April 1813, leaving issue: Mary, born 29 October 1760, married October 1778, Thomas Reed; Daniel, born 1 November 1762, died 21 June 1823, married 23 February 1794, Jane, daughter of Robert and Hannah (Baird) Jamison; Margaret, born 26 March 1766, married 16 March 1784, William Miller;

Nancy, born 11 June 1764, died 15 August 1777; and Richard, born
1 February 1770, died 18 August 1777.[80]

## 12. CAPTAIN JOHN CRAIG

John Craig was one of the three sons of Daniel and Margaret (Brumfield)
Craig. As he deposed in 1820 that he was about 70, his tentative birth
year is established as about 1750.

He entered the service in the summer of 1775 as a volunteer in Captain
William Hendricks' Company, Colonel William Thompson's Pennsylvania
Rifle Battalion, and marched from Easton, Pennsylvania, to Cambridge,
Massachusetts. The troops participated in the invasion of Canada, Hendricks being killed at Québec, 31 December 1775. On 5 January 1776 Craig
was appointed a Second Lieutenant in the Second Pennsylvania Battalion,
and on 11 November 1776, First Lieutenant, Third Pennsylvania Regiment.
On 22 March 1777 he was commissioned First Lieutenant in the Fourth
Continental Light Dragoons, commanded by Colonel Stephen Moylan, the
same unit which his cousin Charles joined three months later.

John Craig and other lieutenants in the Dragoons were evidently dissatisfied with their pay and sent separate letters to General Washington
expressing the opinion that Lieutenants of Horse should have equal pay to
that of Captains of Foot. They threatened to resign if their demands were
not met (November 1777). The General replied with some asperity that he
was not conscious of having said the pay of a Lieutenant of Horse should
be equal to that of a Captain of Foot. He urged them to reconsider their
suggestion that they resign, but added, pointedly, that if they persisted
he would accept their resignations.[81] They elected to remain in the
service.

A few months later, in April 1778, Craig apparently suffered a loss in
rank, for Washington wrote to Colonel Moylan: "I am sorry that this
Gentleman [John Craig] has lost his Rank, because you did not take care
to procure him the Commission of eldest Lieut. . . Mr. Craig . . . says,
that for some time he did duty as eldest Lieut. and that the Rank never
was disputed until the Commissions were issued, and that those officers
who found their Commissions of older dates claimed rank accordingly. . ."[82]

On 21 July 1780 Craig was commissioned a Captain in the Fourth Continental
Dragoons, to rank from 22 December 1778. He continued in service until
the Army was disbanded in 1783.[83]

Although he had been brought up in Bucks County, Captain Craig made
his home in Northampton County after the war. On 27 July 1786, he was
commissioned Lieutenant of Northampton County and his commission was
renewed on 1 September 1791.[84] As County Lieutenant his rank was equivalent to that of Colonel. He was responsible for seeing that the militia
was alerted for service, provided with arms and accoutrements at the
expense of the State, finding substitutes for those men who refused to go
on active service, and assessing and collecting fines. A year following

his appointment a certain John Franklin and others conducted themselves riotously defying the law in Luzerne County, and Charles Biddle, Vice-President of the Supreme Executive Council (the Craigs' great friend) issued a proclamation offering a reward of $400 to anyone "who shall apprehend and secure John Franklin," and lesser amounts for his companions.[85] On 26 September 1787 the Council instructed Colonel Craig (he was so designated) to proceed "with the greatest dispatch" to Wilkes-Barré, taking whatever militia he needed, in order to seize the men named in the proclamation. If Craig succeeded in seizing only Franklin, he was to take no more risks but return his prisoner to Philadelphia.[86] He was successful; on 6 October 1787 Biddle sent an order to David Rittenhouse, State Treasurer, to "Pay to Colonel John Craig or order the sum of three hundred Pounds as a reward for apprehending and securing John Franklin under orders from Council."[87]

John Craig was appointed Collector of Excise for Northampton County on 3 November 1788, and again on 1 September 1791.[88] In April 1793 he was appointed Brigade Inspector of the Brigade composed of the militia of Northampton County.[89]

At a date not yet found, John Craig married his cousin Elizabeth, daughter of Sheriff William and sister of General Thomas and Captains Charles and William Craig.[90] On 30 March 1784 he purchased from William Craig, of Allen Township, miller, and Elizabeth his wife, a tract of land in Allen Township, part of a larger tract which William Craig had inherited from his brother, Thomas Craig, who had died intestate and without issue. The deed showed that William and Thomas were sons of a James Craig who had been granted the land by Thomas and Richard Penn, the Proprietors of Pennsylvania, on 13 February 1753.[91] There is no known relationship between James Craig and Captain John Craig's family. On 13 February 1795 John bought another small tract of land from Robert Craig and his wife Esther. Nine months later (12 November 1795) John Craig, of the Borough of Easton, Esq., and Elizabeth his wife, sold both tracts to John Knecht of Allen Township, yeoman.[92]

In November 1802 Craig became administrator of the estate of Captain Samuel Craig, formerly of the First Pennsylvania Regiment, who should have been related to him, but, as stated at the beginning of this article, no records have been found to show the kinship. He filed his final account on 16 April 1804.[93]

While he was settling the affairs of his former comrade-in-arms, Captain John Craig was himself undergoing physical and financial hardships. He appealed to the United States for relief, and the eminent statesman, Congressman Henry Clay, reported on 24 January 1811 that "when he [Craig] left the service of his country, his constitution was much impaired and injured; he was without the use of his third finger on the right hand which was so contracted as to render that hand and arm an incumbrance; notwithstanding, he forebore to apply to his country for relief; but being now bowed down with old age and infirmity and being poor, and almost helpless, he is compelled to throw himself upon the charity and humanity of his country. . ." By a Congressional resolution, Captain Craig was awarded $1,000.[94]

He also applied to the State for relief; an affidavit, by John Barclay, found in his pension file in the Division of Manuscripts and History, Bureau of Archives and History, at Harrisburg, informs us (28 February 1813): ". . .I well remember Mr. Charles Biddle saying to me that Captain Craig was so poor he could not get from Lancaster until he [Biddle] as Treasurer of the Cincinnati Society had to advance him money. I think I further understood by Mr. Biddle that Society had been obliged to give him money annually for some time previous. That he had no means of supporting himself but what they gave him together with what little he could spare by labour."[95] The Commonwealth of Pennsylvania granted him a pension of $150 per annum.

Soon after the Act of 18 March 1818 was passed, covering Continental Army veterans who were in "reduced circumstances," Captain Craig applied for a pension. He was inscribed on the Pennsylvania Roll at the rate of $22 per month, to commence as of 16 April 1818. In his file is a curious note: "This Pensioner is not worth a Cent; he receives, however, a pension from the State of $150 per annum."

In compliance with the law requiring pensioners to list their holdings, John Craig, then about seventy years old and living at Mount Bethel, Northampton County, filed his statement on 30 November 1820. He said that he owned about 500 acres of unimproved Donation Land in Mercer County, Pennsylvania. It was mortgaged for about $250 with twelve years' interest. He reported that he received a pension of $150 per annum from Pennsylvania. There were no debts due to him that he had hopes of recovering. He owed about $2,500 including the aforesaid mortgage. "I understand that one of my creditors claims $4,000," he said.

On 26 July 1828, when John Craig applied for benefits under the Act of 15 May 1828, he was living at Belvidere, Warren County, New Jersey. He died there, at his son William's home, 29 November 1829.[96] Apparently there was no administration of his estate. It is not known when his wife, Elizabeth (Craig) Craig, died. According to Egle, he left two sons, William and Charles, who married sisters named Mowry (first names not stated).

## 13. LIEUTENANT ROBERT CRAIG

Robert Craig, the last of the Continental Army officers to be considered in this paper, does not seem to have been related to the other officers. He was a son of James Craig, of Allen Township, Northampton County, as shown in a deed, 16 April 1774, whereby James granted to his son Robert a tract of 104 acres in the township.[97] He was a brother of Thomas Craig who died some time before 30 March 1784, and of William Craig, miller, who sold a part of the family property to Captain John Craig, as stated earlier. The published genealogies declare that James Craig was a brother of Thomas Craig, founder of Craig's Settlement, and of Daniel Craig, of Warrington Township, Bucks County, but we have found no documentary evidence to support this assertion. Moreover, the Reverend Richard Webster, who knew the Craigs well, wrote in 1847 that they were not related.

Robert Craig entered the service on 3 November 1776 as a Second

Lieutenant in the Second Canadian Regiment, commanded by Colonel Moses Hazen. Hazen was a New Englander with Canadian connections. His regiment was composed of Canadian refugess, New Yorkers, and Pennsylvanians. On Tuesday, 8 April 1777, the Continental Congress passed a resolution naming Robert Craig and a number of others to be First Lieutenants in "the regiment commanded by Col. Hazen."[98] He must have had some difficulty for in the General Orders at Skippack, 1 October 1777, we read: "Lieut. Robert Cragg (sic) of Col. Hazen's regt. charged with 'Repeated disobediences of orders.' Acquitted."[99] Craig resigned from the service, 1 February 1778.[100]

Robert Craig married Esther Brown, by whom he had six sons: James, Samuel, William, John, Robert, and Joseph.[101] Robert Craig's name is on a list of members of the Warrior Run Presbyterian Church of about 1789.[102] Some time later he and his family moved to Turbutt in Northumberland County, Pennsylvania, where he and his wife Esther (called Hester in the deed) on 13 February 1795 sold the remainder of their Northampton County property to John Craig, Esq., the former captain of Light Dragoons.[103]

Robert died in 1806, not in 1818, as one of the genealogies stated.[104] On 30 September 1806 letters of administration on his estate were granted to Samuel Craig (his son) and James Hammond.[105]

## 14. CONCLUSION

We started out with an enigma: who were the Craigs of Northampton County, Pennsylvania; could the various genealogical accounts be reconciled; and, above all, what relationships, if any, were the Continental Army officers who hailed from Northampton County? We have only partially solved the puzzle. We know that General Thomas, the alleged Paymaster Hugh, Captain Charles, and Captain William, were brothers; and that Colonel Thomas and Captain John were brothers and first cousins once removed of the other four. See Revised Pedigree IV. We have reached the conclusion that Lieutenant Robert belonged to an unrelated family. We have failed so far to establish the identity of Captain Samuel Craig. But we have, at least, placed the Craigs of Northampton County in their historical setting.[106]

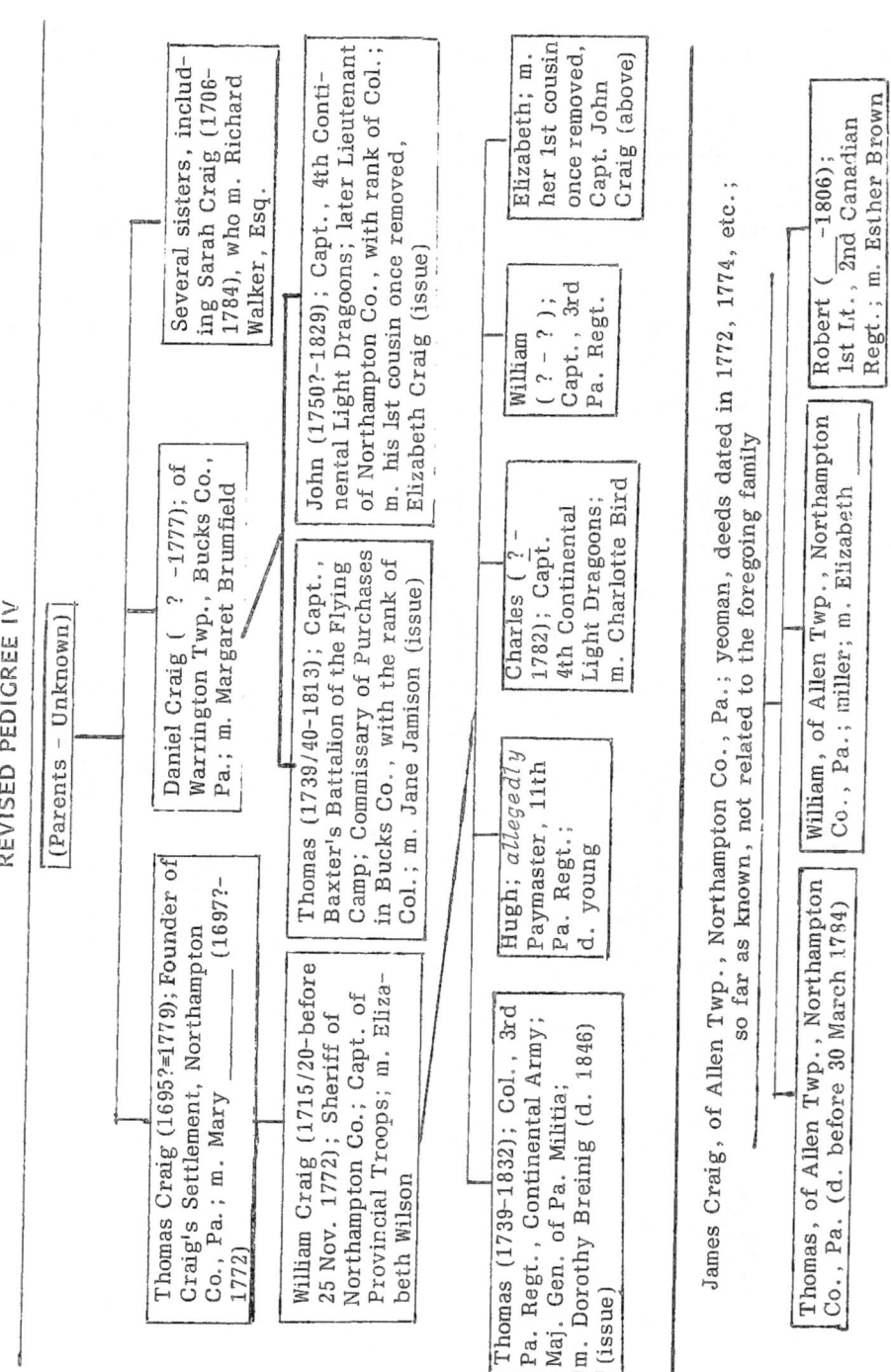

## BIBLIOGRAPHY

[1] Francis B. Heitman, *Historical Register of Officers of the Continental Army during the War of the Revolution, April, 1775, to December, 1783. Reprint of the New, Revised, and Enlarged Edition of 1914. With an Addenda by Robert H. Kelby, 1932.* (Baltimore: Genealogical Publishing Co., 1967.)

[2] Warren S. Ely, "Scotch-Irish Families," *A Collection of Papers Read Before the Bucks County Historical Society*, 2 (1909):523-524, 538-540; Charles Rhoads Roberts, Rev. John Baer Stoudt, Rev. Thomas H. Krick, William J. Dietrich, *History of Lehigh County, Pennsylvania, and Genealogical and Biographical Records of Its Families* (Allentown, Pa., 1914), 2:200-202; Jane Maria Craig, *Samuel Craig, Sr., Pioneer in Western Pennsylvania* (Greensburg, Pa., 1914), pp. 8-10; (Anonymous), *The Scotch-Irish Settlement of Northampton County, Pennsylvania* (published by The Northampton County Historical and Generalogical Society, 1926), pp. 70-73; William Montgomery Clemens, *The Craig Family of Pennsylvania, 1708 to 1895* (Pompton Lakes, N.J., n.d.).

[3] The section on Capt. Samuel Craig is based on the heavily-documented accumulation of materials collected by his descendant, Craig Colgate, Jr., which the writer has examined. His military service is given in his Compiled Service Record cards on microfilm in The National Archives, Washington, D.C.

[4] Carlos E. Godfrey, M.D., *The Commander-in-Chief's Guard During the Revolutionary War* (1904; reprinted by Genealogical Publishing Co., 1972), p. 144.

[5] See Ruth Moser Kistler, "William Allen, Provincial Man of Affairs," *Pennsylvania History*, 1:165-174, and Charles R. Roberts, "William Allen, The Founder of Allentown and His Descendants," *Proceedings of the Lehigh County Historical Society*, i:5-16.

[6] Roberts, *et al., op. cit.*, 2:202.

[7] Northampton County Manuscripts, Historical Society of Pennsylvania, Philadelphia, Pa. Microfilm XR 701.

[8] Bucks Co. Deed Book 10:113-115. All deed and will books cited are on microfilm in The Historical Society of Pennsylvania, but to save space their reel numbers are omitted. Many of the Northampton Co. deed books were consulted in the Courthouse at Easton, especially in a few cases where microfilms were not clear.

[9] Northampton Co. Deeds A-1:17.

[10] Northampton Co. Deeds D-1; 357-359.

## BIBLIOGRAPHY

[11] Dr. Robert Hays Horner, *Northampton County, Pennsylvania Cemeteries*, p. 3. (Typescript, Genealogical Society of Pennsylvania. Hereafter the Genealogical Society will be cited as GSP and the Historical Society of Pennsylvania as HSP.) Thomas and Mary Craig are buried in the Presbyterian Burial Ground, Scotch-Irish Settlement, near Weaversville, Pa.

[12] Thomas Craig's original will, the inventory, and the executor's account are preserved in the Northampton County Archives Building at Easton.

[13] The Rev. Richard Webster, pastor, First Presbyterian Church, Mauch Chunk, Pa., *The Old Church in Allen*, p. 7. Bound in a volume of printed papers entitled, *Historic Pamphlets*, vol. 11, in the Easton (Pa.) Public Library. Mr. Webster's sketches of Allen Township and its pioneers were first published in *The Presbyterian* for 17, 24, and 31 July, and 14 August 1847.

[14] Warren S. Ely, "Scotch-Irish Families," *A Collection of Papers Read Before the Bucks County Historical Society*, 2:538-539.

[15] Bucks Deeds 7:513-514.

[16] Ely, *loc. cit.*, 2:514.

[17] *Ibid.*, 2:530-532.

[18] See especially Northampton Deeds A-1:12 (William Craig to John Potts and Thomas Yorke, recorded 28 Sept. 1753), A-1:16 (William Craig to Edward Scull, 19 Feb. 1752), A-1:14-15 (William Craig to William Logan, 6 Sept. 1753), B-1:121-122 (Peter Fox to William Craig, 4 March 1766).

[19] Matthew S. Henry, *Manuscript History of Northampton County, Pennsylvania* (1851), pp. 93-94 (typescript copy, Easton Public Library). The original manuscript is in HSP, where we saw it after we'd examined the typescript. Parsons' letter is published in *The Papers of Benjamin Franklin*, edited by Leonard W. Labaree and others, Yale University Press, New Haven, 4 (1961):410-411.

[20] *Pennsylvania Archives*, 8th series, 4 (1931):8547. (Hereinafter cited as PA.)

[21] *Ibid.*, 4:3561-3562, 3567, 3571, 3572, 3574, 3575.

[22] Labaree, *op. cit.*, 6 (1963):344.

[23] Original letter of Richard Peters to Thomas Penn is in the Penn MSS., HSP: Official Correspondence, 1756-1757, 8:29-33.

[24] William A. Hunter, *Forts on the Pennsylvania Frontier, 1753-1758* (Harrisburg: The Pennsylvania Historical and Museum Commission, 1960), p. 181.

[25] Northampton County Manuscripts, 1727-1758, p. 185 (HSP, Microfilm XR 698). These manuscripts also reveal that William Craig and William Parsons,

## BIBLIOGRAPHY

"His Majesty's Justices of the Peace in the County of Northampton" were jointly involved in seizing and jailing a number of "disturbers of the peace."

[26]Hunter, *op. cit.*, pp. 221-222.

[27]Labaree, *op. cit.*, 6:393.

[28]Hugh Wilson's estate file (No. 635), Northampton Co. Archives Building.

[29]Northampton Deeds C-1:83-84.

[30]*Ibid.*, C-1:85-86.

[31]*Ibid.*, D-2:617-619.

[32]Charles R. Roberts, "Allen Township, Its Early History and Early Settlers, " *Procs. Lehigh Co. Hist. Soc.*, 1936, p. 76.

[33]Julian P. Boyd and (later) Robert J. Taylor, *The Susquehanna Company Papers* (Ithaca: Cornell University Press: published for the Wyoming Historical and Geological Society, Wilkes-Barré, Pa.), 3 (1930):92-93. (Hereinafter cited as *Susq. Co. Papers.*)

[34]Charles Miner, *History of Wyoming, In A Series of Letters to His Son, William Penn Miner, Esq.* (Philadelphia, 1845), p. 123.

[35]*Susq. Co. Papers*, 4 (1930):40.

[36]John C. Fitzpatrick, editor, *The Writings of George Washington from the Original Manuscript Sources, 1745-1799* (Washington, D.C.: Government Printing Office), 10 (1933):322 and 11 (1934):252, 263, 274, 289, 308.

[37]*Ibid.*, 12 (1934):154, 204.

[38]*Ibid.*, 14 (1936):140.

[39]Anonymous, "Extracts from the Papers of General William Irvine," *The Pennsylvania Magazine of History and Biography*, 5 (1881):275.

[40]*The Journals of the Continental Congress* (Washington, D.C.: Government Printing Office), 25:633.

[41]*Ibid.*, 25:705, 26:242, 28:321-322.

[42]On this debatable matter, Simon Gratz notes: "Thomas Craig (colonel of the Third Pennsylvania Regiment, August 1, 1777. Retired January 1, 1783) and Charles Harrison (colonel of the First Continental Artillery, January 1, 1777, Retired June 17, 1783), though apparently entitled to the brevet rank under the resolution, did not, so far as can be determined, receive it." ("The Generals of the Continental Army in the Revolutionary War." *Pa. Mag. Hist. Biog.*, 27:396.)

[43]*Journals Cont. Cong.*, 25:705. "Deranged" is a military word meaning

## BIBLIOGRAPHY

the troops were declared supernumerary, *i.e.*, no longer needed.

[44]*Ibid.*, 26:242.

[45]Northampton Deeds B-2: 659-660.

[46]William J. Buck, "Col. Thomas Craig," in Moses Auge, *Lives of the Eminent Dead and Biographical Notices of Prominent Living Citizens of Montgomery County, Pa.* (Norristown, 1879), pp. 24-25.

[47]PA, 6th ser., 4:772, 789, and 7:4. The text of his commission as Major General of the 8th Division (comprising the militia of Northampton and Wayne Counties) is in Northampton Deeds C-2: 654-655, dated 17 April 1800.

[48]Lehigh County was created from Northampton County, 6 March 1812. The Borough of Northampton, incorporated 18 March 1811, was formerly called Allentown and resumed its old name in 1838.

[49]In his schedule he wrote dollars and pounds interchangeably.

[50]Henry F. Marx, Librarian, Easton Public Library, compiler, *Marriages and Deaths in Northampton County, 1799-1851. Newspaper Extracts*, 2:484-487.

[51]General Craig apparently had departed from the Presbyterian faith of his forefathers.

[52]Charles J. Ingersoll, *Historical Sketch of the Second War between the United States and Great Britain* (Philadelphia, 1845), 1:86. Ingersoll says, on the same page, "Mr. Rush and I got Mr. Madison to nominate the old soldier to whose memory this passing tribute is devoted without his knowledge, as a brigadier-general in the regular army in 1812; advanced in years as he was, he would have done honor to the station." Either the nomination fell through, or Craig, then a major general of Pennsylvania militia, declined it. Further on, Ingersoll notes that at the peace of 1783, Craig was entitled "to the nominal rank of general," but gives no indication that the Pennsylvanian accepted it. (See note 42.)

[53]Miner, *op. cit.*, p. 123, footnote.

[54]Harriet is mentioned in her father's pension papers as having died on 30 September 1822. *The American Eagle*, of Easton, dated Friday, 11 October 1822, says: "DIED —— In the borough of Northampton Miss *Henrietta* Craig, youngest daughter of General Thomas Craig. The deceased was in the 17th year of her age. . ." (Italics ours.) (Marx, *op. cit.*, 1:104-105.) A Bucks County newspaper also called her Henrietta. (*Marriages and Deaths Copied from The "Bucks County Intelligencer" and its Predecessors*, typescript in GSP; no pagination.)

[55]Single record of Paymaster Craige in the "Return" of the 11th Pennsylvania Regiment, Microcopy 881, Roll 833, The National Archives.

[56]PA, 1st ser., 4:680.

## BIBLIOGRAPHY 35

[57] *Journals Cont. Cong.*, 7:348.

[58] *Ibid.*, 7:353.

[59] Fitzpatrick, *op. cit.*, 10:32.

[60] It's difficult to believe that an "army in great force" could march silently!

[61] John F. Watson, *Annals of Philadelphia and Pennsylvania, in the Olden Time* (Philadelphia, 1898), 2:327.

[62] Anon., *Intelligence in the War of Independence* (Washington, D.C.: Central Intelligence Agency; A Bicentennial Publication, n.d.), p. 35.

[63] Colonel William Allen was a Loyalist officer and son of the Craigs' old friend, Chief Justice William Allen, also a loyal supporter of King George, III.

[64] Washington Papers, Division of Manuscripts, Library of Congress, Microfilm Reel 45.

[65] Washington Papers, LC, MSS Div., microfilm.

[66] Morton L. Montgomery, *History of Berks County in Pennsylvania*, (Philadelphia, 1886), pp. 664 and 894 (account of Mark Bird); Major Harmon Pumpelly Read, F.R.G.S., *Rossiana, Papers and Documents Relating to the History and Genealogy of the Ancient and Noble House of Ross* . . . (Albany, 1908), p. 160.

[67] *Autobiography of Charles Biddle* (Philadelphia, 1883), p. 172 (author's note).

[68] Gratz Collection, Case 4, Box 11.

[69] The William Craig who held all of these offices died before 5 January 1799, when letters of administration on his estate were granted to Daniel Stroud. In November 1799 Stroud reported to the Orphans' Court he had discharged his duties as administrator and asked to be dismissed. (O.C. File No. 23, Folder 1506, Northampton Co. Archives Building, Easton.) In October 1799 the *American Eagle* reported the death of William Craig, in his twelfth year, son of William Craig, deceased, late Prothonotary of Northampton County. (Marx, *op. cit.*, 1:1.)

[70] Biddle. *Autobiography*, p. 216. William Craig's military service record is contained in his Compiled Service Record cards at The National Archives (Microcopy 881, Roll 800), and in PA, 2nd. ser., 10:94 and 448.

[71] Bucks Deeds 25:74-75.

[72] Lists of County Officers, 1752-1852, in Northampton Co. MSS, Microfilm XR701, HSP.

[73] Bucks Deeds 11:250-252.

## BIBLIOGRAPHY

[74] Bucks Wills 3:417-420.

[75] From the family Bible: "Thomas Craig son of Daniel & Mary (sic) was born 27th Feb. 1739" (1739/40?). The entries are evidently copied from the original Bible (date unknown), and Margaret's name misread as Mary. The Bible apparently belonged to Mrs. William M. Gearhart of Norristown, Pa., who corresponded with the local historian and genealogist, Warren S. Ely, in 1905. The transcript is headed: "Record from the Bible of my grand father, Thomas Craig." In another paper she copied "Major Harry Craig Hill's statement made March 24, 1898," in which he gave Daniel's wife's name as "Mary Margaret or Margaret Mary (surname not found)." We know from the records available to us that she was Margaret Brumfield. (Warren S. and Josephine L. Ely Memorial Collection, GSP.)

[76] PA, 2nd Ser., 2:155.

[77] Hannah Benner Roach, "The Pennsylvania Militia in 1777," *The Pennsylvania Genealogical Magazine*, 23 (1964):161-162.

[78] PA, 2nd Ser., 2:556.

[79] PA, 2nd Ser., 10:453.

[80] These names and dates are taken from the family Bible discussed in Note 75. They may or may not be correct.

[81] Fitzpatrick, op. cit., 9:68-69, 82-83.

[82] Ibid., 11:245.

[83] Captain John Craig's military service record is contained on his Compiled Service Record cards in The National Archives, and he discusses it at some length in his application for a pension in 1818 (Microcopy 804, Roll 676).

[84] Northampton Deeds E-1:69 and E-1:699.

[85] *Susq. Co. Papers*, 10:204-205.

[86] Ibid., 10:207. The order concludes: "Council have the utmost reliance on your secrecy and your prudence in conducting the affair. If opposed by force, you are to use force and execute the warrant at all events."

[87] Ibid., 10:225. Craig reported that the Treasurer, "Mr. Rittinghouse," could not pay the $400 at present, but the Surveyor General, John Lukens, said "he would advance the amount to enable me to make a dividend forthwith to the Gentlemen who had Rendred such essential Service to the State, and paid me three hundred pounds accordingly."

[88] Northampton Deeds E-1:531 and E-1:700.

[89] Northampton Deeds B-2:12-13.

[90] William Henry Egle, *Pennsylvania: Genealogies, Chiefly Scotch-Irish and German* (Baltimore: Genealogical Publishing Co., 1969; reprint of the 2nd

# BIBLIOGRAPHY

edition), p. 667 (Genealogy of the Wilson Family). Dr. Egle says John "was not a relative" of Elizabeth, but our researches suggest that they were first cousins.

[91]Northampton Deeds D:198-199.

[92]Northampton Deeds B-2:553-554.

[93]Estate papers of Samuel Craig, Wayne Co. Courthouse, Honesdale, Pa.

[94]John Craig's pension file (S40859), Microcopy 804, Roll 676, The National Archives.

[95]Photocopy of original document is in John Craig's pension file in the Pennsylvania State Archives, Harrisburg.

[96]*Easton Centinel*, Friday, 4 December 1829: "DIED —— On Sunday, November 29th, about 12 o'clock, at the residence of his son, Captain JOHN CRAIG, at the advanced age of 80 years. . ." (Marx, *op. cit.*, 1:309-310.)

[97]Northampton Deeds E-1:264-266.

[98]*Journals Cont. Cong.*, 7:244.

[99]Fitzpatrick, *op. cit.*, 9:297.

[100]Compiled military service record of Robert Craig on cards, The National Archives (Microcopy 881, Roll 80).

[101]Roberts, *et al.*, *op. cit.*, 2:200.

[102]Mrs. Helen P. Burrowes, "The Warrior Run Presbyterian Church," *The Northumberland County Historical Society Proceedings and Addresses* (1939), p. 184.

[103]Northampton Deeds B-2:506-507.

[104]Roberts, *et al.*, *op. cit.*, 2:200.

[105]Northumberland Wills 2:31.

[106]In the course of this study the author has amassed considerable material on the Craigs of Northampton County which was not included in the paper as not being germane to the subject, *i.e.*, the identification and relationships of the Craig officers in the Continental Army. It is planned to place our Craig files and reports in the Library of the National Genealogical Society and xerox copies in the Genealogical Society of Pennsylvania for the use and benefit of Craig descendants.

# INDEX

Abington, Virginia, 7
Albany, New York, 1
Alexandria, Virginia, 3
ALLEN
  John, 15, 19
  Margaret, 9
  William, 4, 9, 14, 20, 21. 23
Allentown, 9
ANTONY, Mark, 18
ARNDT, John, 11

BAIRD, Hannah, 25
BARCKLEY / BARCLAY
  James, 8, 24, 27
  Margaret Craig, 9
  Mary Craig, 24
BARKER, Charles R., 1
BARNHILL
  Elizabeth Potts, 25
  Jane Craig, 24
  John, 24, 25
  Margaret, 25
  Robert, 25
  Samuel, 24
  Sarah Craig, 24, 25
BAXTER
  ____, 5, 30
  William, 25
BEAN, William, 25
BEATTY, Charles, 11, 12
BEISEL, Salome, 5, 18
Belvidere, Warren Co., N.J., 28
Bethlehem, Pa., 13
BIDDLE, Charles, 22, 23, 27, 28
BIRD
  Catherine, 22
  Catherine Van Gezel, 22
  Charlotte, 22, 30
  Gertrude, 22
  Mark, 22
  Rachel, 22
Birdsboro, Pa., 22
Blue Mountain, 12, 17
BOYD
  Jane Craig, 5, 7, 12
  John, 7, 12
  Thomas, 5
Brandywine, 20
BREINIG/BRINIER
  Dorothy, 5, 7, 18, 30

BROADHEAD
  Daniel, 22
BROKAW, Caleb, 16
BROWN
  Elizabeth, 5, 7
  Esther Brown, 5, 7, 29, 30
  Hester, 29
BRUMFIELD, Margaret, 23, 24, 25, 26, 30
BULLOCH, Martha, 25
BUTLER, Richard, 16

Cambridge, Mass., 15, 16
Canada, 12, 15
Church, etcetera
  Presbyterian burial ground, 9
  Lower Towamensing Church, 18
  Presbyterian Church of Neshamity, 11
  Warrior Run Presbyterian Church, 29
  Warwick Meeting House, 11
  Presbyterian Synod, Philadelphia, 6, 8
CLAY, Henry, 27
COLGATE
  Mr., 3, 4
  Craig, Jr., 1, 3
CONGLETON
  William, 10
Colony of Conn., 15
CRAGE, Capt., 20
CRAGG, Robert, 29
CRAIG
  ____, 17
  ____ Kuntz (lady), 5, 6
  ____ Mowry (lady), 28
  ____ Wilson (lady), 12, 15
  Allen, 6
  Ann, 10, 15
  Benjamin, 18
  Catherine Hagenbach/Hagenbuch, 5, 6, 19
  Charles, 3, 4, 5, 10, 15, 17 - 23, 26 - 30

  Charlotte Bird, 22, 30
  Daniel, 5, 8, 9, 11, 23 - 26, 28, 30
  Dorothy Breinig/Brinier, 5, 7, 18, 30
  Eliza, 6, 17, 19
  Elizabeth Brown, 5, 7
  Elizabeth, 9, 10, 15, 27, 28, 30
  Elizabeth Craig, 27, 28, 30
  Elizabeth Wessells, 3
  Elizabeth Wilson, 14, 15, 19, 23, 30
  Ellen, 5
  Esther, 27
  Esther Brown, 5, 7, 29, 30
  Harriet, 5, 19
  Henrietta, 19
  Hester Brown, 29
  Hugh, 4, 10, 15, 19, 24, 29, 30
  James, 5, 7 - 9, 11, 27 - 30
  Jane, 5, 7, 11, 12, 24
  Jane Innis, 3, 4
  Jane Jamison, 25, 30
  Jane Small, 7
  Jean Jamison, 5
  John, 1, 4, 11, 24 - 30
  Joseph, 29
  Margaret Brumfield, 23 - 26, 30
  Margaret, 5, 9 - 12, 15, 25
  Mary, 5, 7 - 11, 15, 19, 24, 25, 30
  Mary Lewin, 24
  Nancy, 25
  Rachel, 4
  Rachel Davies, 3
  Rebecca, 24
  Richard, 25
  Robert, 4 - 7, 27 - 30
  Salome Beisel, 5, 18
  Samuel, 1, 3, 4, 5, 7, 27, 29
  Samuel Davies, 3
  Sarah, 10, 11, 15, 24, 25, 30
  Thomas, 1, 3 - 19, 22 - 25, 27 - 30

# INDEX

"a" Thomas, 25
William, 1, 4 - 15, 19, 22 - 24, 27 - 30
CRAIGE
\_\_\_\_, Paymaster, 19
David, 11

DARRACH, Lydia, 20
DAVIES
  Benjamin, 3
  Rachel, 3
DAVIS, Evan, 10
Donation Land, Mercer Co., Pa., 28
Dublin, Ireland, 8, 15
Dungannon, Ireland, 5, 8

Easton, Pa., 1, 3, 18, 23, 26, 27
EPPLER, Andrew, 19

Fort:
  Allen, 13
  Bingham, 12
  Hamilton, 13
  Washington, 25
Founder of the Christian Faith, 18
FOX, Peter, 14
Frankford, 20
FRANKLIN
  Benjamin, 8, 12, 13
  John, 27

GATES, Horatio, 18, 21
GORDON, John, 3
GRAHAM, Joseph L., 1
GRAY/GREY
  James, 11
  Jean, 11
  John, 5, 11, 12
  Margaret Craig, 5, 11, 12

HAGENBUCH/HAGENBACH
  Andrew, 14
  Catherine, 5, 6, 14, 19
  Margaret, 14
HAMILTON, James, 13
HAMMOND, James, 29
Harrisburg, Pa., 1, 28
HAYS, John, 10
HAZEN, (Moses), 4, 29

HECKMAN
  Charles, 6
  Eliza Craig, 6
HENDRICK, William, 26
HERRON, Thomas, 10
HORSFIELD
  Timothy, 13
HULING, John, 23
HUMPTON, Richard, 19

INNIS, Jane, 3, 4
Ireland, 4, 8
IRVINE, William, 16

JANE, 4
JAMES, Abel, 20, 21
JAMESON/JAMISON
  Hannah Baird, 25
  Henry, 24, 25
  Jane, 25, 30
  Jean, 5
  Mary, 25
  Robert, 25
JENNINGS, John, 14, 15
JONES, John, 13

KERR, William, 10
KLINE
  John, 17
  Juliana, 17
KNECHT, John, 27
KRAEMER
  Daniel, 17, 19
  Eliza Craig, 17, 19
KUNTZ, \_\_\_\_ (lady), 5, 6

Landsdowne, Pa., 1
LATTIMORE
  Robert, 10
LEE, Capt. \_\_\_\_, 20
Lehigh Water Gap, 9, 18
LOGAN, William, 9
LUST, Thomas, 25

Mauch Chunk, Pa., 6
MIFFLIN, Thomas, 17
Military (Engagements)
  Associators, Warrington Twp., Bucks Co., 25
  Battalion:
    2d Pa., 4, 15, 23 26
    of the Flying Camp, 5, 25, 30
    (Pa.) Rifle, 26

Dragoons:
  Light, 29
  4th Continental (Light), 4, 20, 26, 30
  3d Pa., 4
  4th Pa., 4
Infantry, 1st Continental, 4, 19
Life Guards, 3, 4
Militia:
  Brigade, of Northampton Co., 27
  2d Div., Bucks and Montgomery Co., 17
  7th Div., Pa., 6
Provincial, 13
Regiment:
  2d Canadian, 4, 29, 30
  1st Pa., 3, 4, 27
  3d Pa., 4 - 6, 15, 16, 22, 23, 26, 30
  5th Pa., 3
  9th Pa., 4, 25
  10th Pa., 19
  11th Pa., 4, 19, 30
  Pa. Rifle, 19
  Pa. Riflemen, 15
Battles:
  Brandywine, 3, 16
  Edgehill, 20
  Germantown, 16
  Long Island, 3
  Monmouth, 16
  Paoli, 3
  Short Hills, 16
  Trenton, 3
Invasion:
  of British Colony, 15
  of Canada, 18, 26
Mutiny of Pa. Line, 3
Valley Forge, 3, 16
Wars:
  1812, 8th Div., 17
  Yankee-Pennamite, 15
MILLER
  Capt. \_\_\_\_, 19
  Abraham, 19
  Margaret Craig, 25
  William, 25

# INDEX

**MOLYNEAUX**
 Frederick, 3
 Morristown, N.J., 16
 Mount Bethel, North-
  ampton Co., 28
**MOWRY,** ___ (lady), 28
**MOYLAN**
 Stephen, 20, 26

Nebraska, 6
Neshaminy, Bucks
 Co., Pa., 11
New York, 3, 25
**NICHOLSON,** John, 3
Norristown, Philadel-
 phia Co., 17
Northampton, Lehigh
 Co., Borough of, 17

**PARSONS**
 William, 8, 9, 12, 13
**PENN**
 ___, 15
 Richard, 15
 Thomas, 13, 15, 27
 William, 27
Pennsylvania, 4, 7,
 16, 17, 25, 28
**PETERS,** Richard, 13
Philadelphia, 1, 2, 6,
 9, 12 - 14, 20,
 21 - 23, 27
**POTTS,** Elizabeth, 25

Quebec, 26

**RALSTON,** John, 10
**READ/REED**
 George, 22
 Gertrude Bird, 22
 Mary Craig, 25
 Thomas, 25
Reading, Berks Co.,
 Pa., 21, 22
Richmond, Va., 1
**RICKEY,** John, 25
**RITTENHOUSE**
 David, 27
**ROBINSON,** William, 25
**ROOSEVELT**
 Anna Eleanor, 25
 Anna Eleanor Roose-
  velt, 25
 Cornelius Van
  Schaick, 25
 Elliott, 25
 Franklin Delano, 25

 Margaret Barn-
  hill, 25
 Martha Bullock,
  25
 Theodore, 25

**ST. CLAIR**
 Arthur, 15
**SCIPIO,** 18
Scotland, 7, 8
**SCOTT**
 Robert, 24
 William, 24
**SCULL,** Nicholas, 9
Settlements:
 Craig's, 1, 3 - 6,
  8, 12, 14, 23,
  28 - 30
 Irish, 4, 13
 Scotch-Irish, 1, 4,
  9
**SMALL,** Jane, 7
Society, Cincinnati, 28
South Carolina, 3, 16
Stemblerscille, Towa-
 mencing Twp., 6
Stenton, Northern
 Liberties of Pa., 9
**STEPHENSON**
 Hugh, 24
 Rebecca Craig, 24
**STEWART**
 Charles, 24
 John, 24
 Patrick, 10
Stirlingshire,
 Scotland, 5, 8
**STONE**
 Walter Jenifer, 22
Stroudsburg, Monroe
 Co., 13

**TAYLOR**
 Ann, 14
 Ann Craig, 15
 James, 14, 15
**THOMPSON**
 ___, 19
 Catherine Bird, 22
 William, 3, 15, 19,
  22, 26
Turbutt, Northumber-
 land Co., Pa., 29
Tuscarora Valley,
 Juniata Co., near
 Ft. Bingham, 12

**VAN GEZEL**
 Catherine, 22
Valley Forge, 3, 16
Virginia, 7
**WAGGONER**
 Widow ___, 21
**WALKER**
 Ann, 11
 Richard, 5, 10, 11, 25,
  30
 William, 11
Warrington, Bristol Road
 in Village of, 11
**WASHINGTON**
 Gen. ___ 4, 16, 18, 20,
  21, 26
 Maj. ___, 21
Washington, D.C., 1
**WATSON,** ___, 20
Weaversville, Pa., 5, 7, 9
**WEBSTER**
 Rev. (Richard), 11, 14,
  15, 19, 28
**WESSELS,** Elizabeth, 3
West Virginia, now,
 Kanawha Co., 3
White Plains, 19
Wilkes-Barre, 27
**WILSON**
 Elizabeth, 14, 19, 23. 30
 Hugh, 12 - 15
 James, 22
 Rachel Bird, 22
 Samuel, 14
 Thomas, 14
**WILT,** Abraham, 21
**WISTAR/WISTER**
 Caspar, 8, 9, 14, 15
 Catherine, 14
**WOOD,** Joseph, 16
Wyoming Valley, Luzerne
 Co., 15

**YEAGER,** Rev. Mr. ___, 18
York Town (York),
 Pa., 3, 16, 21


## ROYALTY

James I, 5
Lord Cornwallis, 16

www.ingramcontent.com/pod-product-compliance
Lightning Source LLC
Chambersburg PA
CBHW061517040426
42450CB00008B/1659